Two Car

and a Plan:

Retiring Early as Full-Time Nomads

CHRIS ENGLERT

Walking Platform Press

Copyright © 2023 EatWalkLearn Publishers

Walking Platform Press, an imprint of EatWalkLearn Publishers

226 Rainbow Drive #12659

Livingtson, TX 77399

www.EatWalkLearn.com

ISBN: 9798441518475

Walking Platform Press First Edition

For information about special discounts, bulk purchases and book club assistance, contact hello@eatwalklearn.com

The EatWalkLearn Speakers Bureau can bring speakers to your authors to your live event. Contact the EatWalkLearn Speakers Bureau at hello@EatWalkLearn.com

Library of Congress Cataloging-in-Publication Data:

Names: Englert, Chris, author

Title: Two Carry-Ons and a Plan/Chris Englert

Description: Texas: Walking Platform Press [20203 ¦ Summary: "An early-retired couple travels the world full-time with two carry-on suitcases and provides their love story of how they created a plan and sold everything to leave the USA and discover the world." Provided by Publisher.

Subjects: Adventure Travel. Retirement. Travel Planning.

DEDICATION

To all the people in the world who are looking for adventure, especially to Kelly, who I wish the best adventure of all.

CONTENTS

Retiring as a Full-time Traveling Nomad

Welcome. You've heard about it. Dreamed about it. Wondered about it. And now, you're ready to seriously consider it. But what is "it?"

It's retirement on the move. Exploring the world, enjoying each day, moving intentionally, improving yourself, learning about others. Relaxing into the next phase of your life that doesn't include a home. Nor an RV. Or maybe even a car. It's a time when you might not own walls, tables, mugs, or garages.

For us, this story is our nomad story. It's about how we took an idea that turned into a dream that turned into an action plan that turned into our daily life. It's our nomad life. For us, that means we travel full-time with two roller bags and two backpacks. With us is everything we own. This story is how we live our lives. We hope it inspires you to do the same. We're here to tell you how to make your traveling nomad retirement dreams a reality.

What Is Nomad Life?

Nomad Life, as we define it, is a lifestyle undertaken by individuals who want to move about the world in a minimalist manner, seeing as much as they can, one location at a time.

Some nomads travel solo, some travel as couples, and others travel as families. "Digital nomads" travel the world using their computers to generate income. This might be you, but it's not us and that is not our story. Our revenue comes from a life-time of planning and saving.

What Is Full-Time Travel?

We believe a full-time traveler is someone who moves about the world, not necessarily anchored to any location for any length of time, whose home is where the heart is.

Who Are We?

We're Chris (me, the wife) and Steve (the husband), a couple on the move. Our kids are grown and our careers are completed. We are full-time travelers exploring the world, one month at a time. We retired early; Chris at 49 and Steve at 61.

How We Got to Retirement

We are a newer couple, having been married just ten years. We came to our retirement from different paths with different financial goals.

We make it sound easy to get financially ready to retire. It's not. We made good and bad decisions along the way, indulging when we should have sacrificed, and sacrificing when we should have indulged. But the point is, we both had plans. We followed them as well as we could, and we got there, roughly on the timeline we laid out. People who retire all have one thing in common. They had a plan, made it work, and retired. We won't go into financial retirement strategies here. There are many books and experts to help you plan your retirement. Our expertise is how to live your retirement as a traveling nomad.

We're thrilled to tell you how we're living our life. We'll not only tell our story, but we'll also give you hints, tips, tricks and to-do lists for every step of the way so you can make your nomad retirement dreams a reality. Let's start with our story.

This is the greatest love story ever told. Chris, the "I" voice in the beginning of the story, takes over from here.

A Love Story

I'm going to tell you the greatest love story ever told. Like any good love story might, ours begins with divorce.

Actually, it starts a few years before the first marriage.

And maybe even before that.

A First Love Develops

This love story begins in the backseat of my parents' sedan, whichI shared with my older sister. We hated each other in the way only sisters can, but on the road-trips-from-hell that my parents forced upon us, we became partners. To tolerate endless hours of driving as fast as Dad and Mom could to get to Point A so we could return as fast as we could to Point B, we played endless games of *I Spy* and *License Plate Bingo*. The hum of hundreds of miles of American asphalt tried to lull us to sleep, but we *had* to stay awake.

"Dammit," Dad would say, "I didn't work my tail off all year for a two-week vacation that you girls sleep through." As punishment for sleeping through the amber waves of grain passing by, he'd toss us out of the car to run on the interstate's shoulder before we could re-enter the car, a mile up the road. By the time we ran the fearful mile, we were wide awake again.

Despite this, or maybe because of it, my love of travel was born. By our early teens, my sister and I had stayed awake through 35 states. I found joy in the trips by writing about our antics, my spiral notebook filled with a narrative of snarky comments, unsent postcards, and torn admission ticket stubs. Cut up AAA maps and TripTik pages highlighted our routes. This first love, the one for travel writing, began on interstate 5 in California.

That's the start of one love story. And here's the start of another.

A Second Love Develops

By my early 20s, I had traveled to every US state and the District of Columbia. My Dad's vigorous comments, "See the US first!" rang like a chorus of crickets in a Kansas corn patch. Work travel took me to the big cities; money from work took me to the national parks. I ticked them all off, then I started on the rest of the world. By 30, my tally trued up to over 40 countries.

In 1999, the world fretted over its doom. People feared the ticking of the last second of the century and its implosion of all of its computers by the Y2K drama. Me, on the other hand, I had a different pro-tech vision.

I envisioned the creation of a single, magical device. This fantastic hand-held tool would be able to do five things:

1. Make phone calls
2. Get on the internet
3. Navigate
4. Read email
5. Contain a personal-defense system like a stun gun or pepper spray

Recall that in 1999, these terrific hand-held devices had just emerged from their 5-pound bags, and they made phone calls poorly. But I reasoned that if this magical device showed up by 2005, I would take it and myself around the world on a year-long traveling adventure. The travel itch that had prickled in the back of the family sedan still needed scratching.

My 33rd birthday rang in the way a good *Sex in the City Girl* might enjoy. A morning date with one fella, and an evening date with another. The day after my 33rd birthday, I woke up and decided it was time to get married.

A flashy Love@AOL internet post garnered the attention of my first husband. He was dreamy and adventurous and fun. He sailed, dreamed romance in the stars, and the future in the skies. We got engaged, started new careers, and got married.

And this is where I *thought* two love stories would meld. We'd travel, I'd write, and we'd grow old together in a traveling sort of way.

I shared with him my magical 2005 vision of world travel. He wanted nothing to do with it; he couldn't fathom taking off a year from his career.

Suddenly, he was not dreamy, was not adventurous, and was not fun.

After seven years of stormy weather, the day came when he sailed one way, I hiked the other. Our beautiful 4-year old daughter rode the ebb and flow of our new life and its transitions with me.

My vision where my first love of travel writing interweaved with my second love of a romantic partner persisted. But now custody rules and regulations kept my daughter and me grounded in the US. My life of world travel would have to wait.

The two love stories festered.

The Love Stories Merge

In 2009, after two years of single-mom adventures, a dashing man of desire and dare dangled his smile and smarts my way. On our first date, sparks flew. But this time, the first date wasn't about discussing the building of a family and the growth of careers. After assuring me that he'd accept my daughter and me as a package, my second question to my darling date was about which airline he liked to travel.

And he answered, with the perfect most answer ever to come my way.

Steve said, without missing a beat, "In the US, Southwest. Worldwide, Delta. Why?"

And that's when my dream–living a travel life with the love of my life in the best love story ever told– got its heartbeat. Could I travel the world and share it with someone who would enjoy it, too? The dormant seed I had planted in my heart back in 1999 vibrated to life.

Our First International Trip Together

While dating, Steve and I wanted to take a trip. Deciding where to go was a bit of a challenge. While I had been to 50+ countries by this point, Steve had only been to a handful. Don't get me wrong, he loved to travel, but his travel had been built around a family of four and a small business. He hadn't had many opportunities to get abroad. Whereas he wanted to do Western Europe's top ten like Paris, London, and Madrid, I had already checked those off my list.

He mentioned that he always wanted to visit Israel. "Israel?" I thought. Never even considered it. Some quick googling found us an amazing deal on Gate 1 travel that included our air, hotels, most meals, and all tours. By booking an all-inclusive tour, it took some of the pressure off of both of us for endless details.

On the Israeli trip through Masada, Tel Aviv, Jerusalem, Bethlehem, the Golan Heights, the West Bank and Cesaria, we learned that we were "travel compatible." We fell into step quickly with each other, solving logistics challenges easily, overcoming travel obstacles with smiles, and giggling our way through insane security lines and bureaucratic rules. Even on the plane, things worked smoothly. Not only did he love the aisle seat and I loved the window, we couldn't fathom checking our luggage or carrying heavy bags. Our travel philosophies matched like peanut butter and jelly.

For my 44 ½ birthday, we took our first trip to Europe. On this trip, we enjoyed the Western European countries that neither of us had visited: Hungary, Austria, Prague, and Germany. By this time, we had been dating about a year, and we had agreed we wanted to get married. But we weren't engaged yet.Steve flat out told me that he didn't want to propose on this trip. He didn't want the pressure of it,nor the responsibility of hiding an engagement ring from me for a week. He set my expectations low, and off we went to explore four new countries.

In Budapest, we swirled in a Hungarian hot tub, laughing in our Soviet-style bathing suits rented from the bath house lady. Afterwards, we joined 300,000 of our closest friends in Heroes Square to have Rod Stewart serenade us with *Do You Think I'm Sexy?* We crashed that night in a Marriott on the Danube River, getting a taste for a life we'd fall in love with.

At the time, we had corporate jobs which rewarded us with hotel points, and we hacked those points for great stays at Marriotts throughout Europe. Little did we know at the time that hacking travel would become a hobby in the future.

By the time we got to Prague, I knew for sure I wanted to marry this man. We were soul mates. On my half birthday, a day I celebrate because my "full birthday" is sandwiched between Christmas and New Years and which everyone forgets, we awoke. I remember the first thing Steve said to me that day which set up a day I'll always remember. He said, "Happy Half Birthday. It's going to be a fantastic day!" Not that those comments were truly exceptional, but the way he said "fantastic" set my heart all a-twitter and made me wonder if he were, in fact, going to propose on that day.

We journeyed through Prague, its castles, rose gardens, and bridges. We cried our way through Josef as we found some of Steve's ancestors' names painted on the temple walls. By the time we got to the astronomical clock, our emotions hung by a thread. We needed a laugh so we attended a puppet show.

The show finished at 10 pm. Famished, we joined the throng of late-night dinner at a Spanish place I'd chosen. At dinner, Steve looked into my eyes, told me he loved me and that he wanted to spend the rest of his life with me. And that was it.

That was it! Here I thought he had fooled me and was actually going to propose. And then he didn't.

But then, with a few minutes left before the clock struck midnight, Steve paid the bill and invited me to look at the amazing astronomical clock again. We walked over to admire it. He was behind me. I looked up at the clock, pointing out all of its features, oohing and ahhing, and not paying attention to him. Little did I know, he was behind me, on bended knee, waiting for me to turn around.

I continued to blah blah blah. Then he said, "Honey, look what I found!" to get me to turn around. Shocked, I found him on his knee, ring box open, love in his eyes. In the meantime, a crowd of about 20 Korean tourists surrounded us. They broke out in song to Queen's, *We Are the Champions*, as Steve asked me to marry him while the clock struck midnight.

The "Yes!" The hug. The kiss. The cheers! We were engaged!

A year later, we cruised to Alaska with family members for the wedding. In Juneau, we hired a one-man show to marry us. He picked up the wedding party in a limo, chauffeured us to the Juneau courthouse to get our marriage license, had us don special ice boots, flew us in helicopter to the top of the Mendenhall Glacier, gave us a bouquet and boutonniere, married us, popped us a bottle of champagne, photographed us, cheered us with fresh glacier water, and then whisked us back to our cruise ship to depart four hours later. Our wedding was the signature to a life we had begun together of adventure, thrills, and love.

Married Life Begins

Steve and I settled back into our corporate jobs, raising my youngest and parenting his older son and daughter. As we could fit in unusual travel options, we did. Two years into marriage, we took on another adventure. We purchased around-the-world airline tickets to circumnavigate the globe in 30 days. From Denver to Stockholm to Athens to Moscow to Beijing to LA to Mexico to Utah, we crammed the world into our pockets, ticking off as much adventure as we could. No matter how much we traveled, we couldn't get enough and we quickly realized that travel was a lifestyle we loved and in which we thrived. How could we do it more?

Our youngest had seven more years until high school graduation. In the meantime, we began to think about life after her graduation. Would we retire? Could we? What would it look like? We batted around the idea of owning four places in our retirement, one for each season. We thought about long-term "timeshare type" schemes where we could move four times a year without owning anything. We considered buying a small place to run as a rental until we came off the road. We thought about RVs, vans, and even the Peace Corps. We *never* thought about living on a golf course in Florida.

Our corporate lives continued. I continued to sell college textbooks, and he continued to sell educational software. We got our globetrekking highs by cashing-in business travel perks and going on long weekend trips. Neither one of us loved the constant grind of business travel in and out of Denver, but we did love accumulating the travel points and travel status that came with frequent weekly trips. Yet, the go-go-go of business and vacation travel (where you have to squeeze everything in) were the only types of travel we knew. We were good at it. Yet even though we did want to continue to travel, we also knew that we didn't want to maintain the crazy pace and rhythm in retirement. There had to be a better way.

While we finished out our careers and graduated our youngest, we both continued to research options for retirement. We also looked to our parents for ideas. Steve's parents retired to Florida while mine had retired to more entrepreneurship. None of the options appealed to us, but we really didn't know what exactly we wanted. It wasn't *Nomadland* like the movie, nor was it digital nomad life or even van life. What model *could* we follow?

The Finances of Our Nomad Life

Meanwhile, we looked at our finances. Regardless of the retirement model we'd use, how could we pay for our dream of world travel? Even though we didn't quite understand what it would look like, we knew we had work to do on our finances. Steve and I met when I was 42 and he was 48. We had both selected different paths to retirement. We wanted to get on the same page with our retirement finances, but we weren't sure how to do it.

Maybe you're like me: I reached retirement early because I started early. At 22, I immediately began socking away as much money as I could when I was fresh out of grad school, taking advantage of 401Ks, sales bonuses, and matching company funds. Or you may be like Steve, in the last decade of his career, took advantage of his highest earning years and squeezed money by the bucket full into his retirement accounts while at the same time reducing his expenses.

Reconciling "his" portfolio and "my" portofolio took some work. A financial planner helped us assess how to rebalance things, manage our tax responsibilities, and get Steve to his retirement number quicker. By paying off the house, Steve could also funnel most of his highest earning years right into his retirement portfolio. This strategy accelerated his gains while at the same time reducing some portfolio risk for me. It was a win-win.

Because I had planned from the beginning of my career to retire early, when the chance came, I took it at age 49. My industry was going through growing pains. College textbooks no longer filled a niche at universities due to the rise of the internet and direct-to-consumer buying strategies. Although I had planned to retire at 55, I called my financial planner to talk through an earlier retirement. The entire conversation took ten minutes. As long as I made $100 a month for the next six years, I'd not only hit my financial goals, I'd exceed them. Realizing I wouldn't have to suffer through corporate downsizing, restrategizing, and reprioritizing new market conditions, I resigned the very next day. I figured I could dog walk for $100 a month if necessary.

Instead of dog walking, I dabbled and started a small publishing company dedicated to hiking content, created a couple of websites, and produced four books. I became well-known in Denver's hiking community. I had more fun in five years as a small publisher than I ever did working in corporate America! Yet, even though I was having great fun changing the Denver hiking scene, I was in waiting mode. Steve needed to retire and our youngest needed to graduate high school.. But in the meantime, although I was in control of my own schedule, I was anxious to see the rest of the world.

In 2018, the perfect storm of opportunity came our way. Our daughter, eager to enjoy the world on her terms, signed up for Rotary International's Study

Abroad program. She got accepted to study in Brazil for a year. With tears streaming, we put her on a plane at the age of 15 ½ to go off and have a full-blown adventure of her own. After I dried my tears and settled into her absence, I grew restless.

In the meantime, Steve started a new job. He loved it, and he also quickly learned that he wouldn't be able to vacation in the spring. His sales goals required going full-speed ahead from February to May. I was crushed! All along I was thinking we'd be able to dash off for three-day weekends and enjoy a nice spring break without the pressures of a teenager at home. It was not to be.

And then the science of Google always listening in, I got an ad on my computer for a company called Remote Year. This company pitched an interesting experience that tugged at my adventure spirit. I could sign up for their four-month program where I could travel Latin America, live for a month each in four different cities, practice my Spanish, and be surrounded by fun and interesting people. They'd take care of the logistics. All I had to do was show up.

How would I break the news to Steve of my idea to vacate him during his busiest times of work? Would he see the idea as one where I was shirking our marriage or one that would strengthen our ideas of a future life? I sent him a calendar invite for date night and mentioned that I had an idea I wanted to discuss. He accepted the invite, and that evening, we sat down for dinner. The conversation went like this:

Me: "Honey, I have an idea."
Steve: "What time do I drop you off at the airport?"

He knew. He knew me. He knew us. He knew that me going to Latin America would be healthy for us both. Yes, we'd miss each other. But he knew that if I couldn't travel, I'd be miserable, and if he were going to be swamped at work, I should jump at the opportunity. Plus, what would I learn that I could bring back into our conversation about our retirement plans? He was all for it.

I signed up for Remote Year the next day. Together with a group of 43 other people, we traveled to four Latin American countries for four months. We found Airbnb apartments and shared them amongst ourselves, each person guaranteed a room of her own. In each city, we had work space at places like WeWork, and a local go-to person to help us sort out day-to-day items like haircuts, gyms, doctors, and entertainment. We lived in each community for a month, enjoying white water rafting in Santiago, Chile; hiking through the coffee regions of Medellin, Colombia; finding pink-toed tarantulas and mouse-size monkeys in the Amazon in Lima, Peru; and working out with the Lucha Libre Luchadores in Mexico City, Mexico.

When each month finished, we flew to the next location to do it all again. As we traveled in a group, we developed friendships, embedded ourselves in the local communities, worked our jobs, and explored the world. This 30-day-at-a-time model opened up my eyes to how retirement could work. It was the first time I thought about how our "Nomad Life" might really be possible.

During this period, Steve and I missed each other greatly. We'd WhatsApp often, giving virtual kisses at night and texting good mornings each day. Steve continued to crush it at work, eventually winning Rookie of the Year! At the same time, never one to sit still while detesting time alone, he turned our house into an Airbnb. He became an Airbnb Superhost and quickly learned the ins and outs of the Airbnb platform and what travelers look for. He met guests who stayed, not just for a day or two, but weeks at a time. Soon, we both started having epiphanies.

While watching the Peruvian sun set over gorgeous landscapes, I suddenly realized two things: the infrastructure to build for our retirement and the answer to the question of life. The infrastructure would be built around slow travel of 30 days at a time and the answer to the question of life was to share life with someone else.

At the halfway point of my Latin America adventure, Steve finagled his way to Panama for a weekend. After a few kisses, words jumped out of our mouths. I shared everything with him that I had learned about slow travel, and he braindumped his knowledge about Airbnbs. Light bulbs burst. We were onto something! Had we found the way to structure our retirement?

The weekend ended, and we returned to our respective places. Steve finished out his sales season, and I finished out my Remote Year commitment. I returned to the States and reunited with Steve. Shortly afterward, our daughter returned from Brazil.

If our thoughts had been on fire in Panama, they exploded in Denver. Combining everything from Remote Year and everything from Steve's Superhosting experience, all of a sudden, we understood the "how" of our future nomad life. We would slow travel. Instead of dashing every week to some place new, we'd plan to chunk our travel into 30-day blocks of time. By moving slowly, we'd enjoy more areas and eliminate frequent transit expenses. And immediately, we started to truly plan.

The Planning Stage

Steve and I pored over websites for ideas. We created lists upon lists, from countries where we wanted to go to places we wanted to visit to dream destinations. We fleshed out our vision of what retirement would look like. Slow travel and thirty-day stays became the jigsaw pieces to our idea. We knew we never wanted to live in snow and cold again. 72 degrees would be our ideal temperature to thrive.

Even though we could envision the how, what, and where, we couldn't figure the when. We had so many unresolved questions that we couldn't actually plan an itinerary. The major question in our departure plans revolved around our daughter who would be graduating high school the month before we wanted to depart. Where she decided to go to college would influence a few things: would we need to domicile in the state she selected for college? Would we take her to college as part of our departure itinerary?

As she went through college admissions roulette, we formulated a variety of scenarios and put tentative departure plans into place. Those scenarios included investing in a place for her to live near campus, picking our domicile from a list of states if she picked a public school, and domiciling in Texas if she picked a private school or went to college internationally. Despite the different scenarios, here is what we knew as solid decisions: we'd sell the house, we'd depart in the summer, and we would not have a storage unit. Decisions and plans swirled daily. Finally, one weekend when things were way too chaotic in our lives with the randomness of choice and uncertainty, I had

had enough. I scheduled a quiet weekend getaway for us up in the Colorado mountains to chill and enjoy the changing of the Aspen leaves.

At eighteen months before departure, Steve and I settled into the cabin in the woods for a weekend and really started thinking about how our life would look. We created a long list of the countries we wanted to visit. Having traveled to over 60 countries already, I wasn't too keen on revisiting some places, but Steve on the other hand, hadn't been to them and wanted to go. We put together a spreadsheet of the cities within those countries and then researched the time of year their temperatures would match our 72-degrees goal (email us if you want to see the spreadsheet.)

We sorted, highlighted, deleted, and rearranged. We asked ourselves if these locations were places we might want to live or were they just places we wanted to visit. We tried to prioritize the list to the possible places we'd want to live. Soon, we had a general idea of where we wanted to go and a rough itinerary for our route. It laid upon a two-year timeline of roughly twenty places. We figured two years would be enough time to see all the places we wanted to see and give us an idea of where would be a good place to settle. We didn't know it at the time, but two years was never going to be enough time.

With US passports, we are lucky enough to be able to travel fairly freely throughout the world without securing visas. Or, if we need visas, they're generally easy to get and readily affordable. There are a few countries, though, like China and Russia, that require many hoops to jump. We vaguely paid attention to this as we set forward possible itineraries, and when we finally made it out and on the road, we paid much more attention to visa requirements, particularly those for Europe and the Schengen district.

Our itinerary looked like this. We'd leave the US, go to Central America, make our way through South America, jump over to Australia and New Zealand, hop to South Africa, and then roam through Europe, ultimately ending up in Portugal. Along the way, we hoped we would find a place for us to live long term if it wasn't going to be the US.

Once we had our itinerary, we finalized the dates for the big decisions; selling our house, getting a safe deposit box, domiciling in Texas (more on this later), buying our plane tickets, disposing of our stuff, packing our carry-ons, and heading out to a life of full-time traveling nomads. In one focused weekend, we planned the launch of our retirement and its adventure.

All indicators pointed to a date when Steve could retire, and our daughter would graduate from high school. While Steve continued in his full-time job, I would begin researching and working through the planning necessary to get us out of our house and into the world. How would we live within the budget we set, get to all the places we wanted to see, enjoy our best life, and live our life affordably?

About this time, we made some new friends who lived in Denver who were also on a similar path as ours. Through their website and vlog, Go With Less, we learned a few more tricks to get to our nomad life. One trick was house sitting, and credit card hacking for real. Together with Airbnb, we could build a travel lifestyle of 30-day stays and stretch our dollar further by housesitting and credit card hacking.

Armed with this new information, Steve and I honed our nomad retirement plan, adjusting our budget and timeline. If we could buy down our accommodation budget through housesitting and stretch our travel budget through credit card hacking, how would that change our budget and timeline? Steve was thrilled. Whereas he had concerns about our overall expenses more than I did, when he embraced the magic of housesitting and credit card hacking, his anxiety lowered. The third and fourth pieces of our nomad puzzle popped right in. Our nomad life was made up of 30-day stays, Airbnb accommodations, housesitting and credit card hacking.

By the way, what's this love story? It's a story of two people, well-matched, falling in love with each other and themselves as we travel the world doing what we love and living our best lives. At this point in our journey, love floated through us as we made each decision. Although there was stress and anxiety about tough decisions, we knew we were well matched and tracking toward each other on a journey of adventure.

We could see a way forward, and we were on our way out the door.

Putting It All Together

After lots of conversation and jiggering of the puzzle pieces, we ruled out many things and settled on a short to mid-term plan looked like this:

Timeline: Travel fulltime for at least two years

Budget: Stick to an affordable budget of $48000 annually (see below)

Type of travel: Travel lightly with one carry-on and one backpack each

Accommodation: Stay one month or more at a time in one location

                   Pay for that stay through one of three ways:

            1. Housesitting

2. Airbnb, VRBO or other short-term rental options

3. Credit card travel hacking

Mode of travel: Travel between locations via plane, train, car, or boat

Finance travel through one of two ways

1. Purchase with dollars

2. Purchase with miles from either our frequent flyer accounts or credit card points

Community building: Embed in the community by

Doing walking tours

Joining walking/hiking groups

Taking language courses

Exercising in the local gyms/community centers

Shopping in local markets

Volunteering

Interacting in social media groups

With eighteen months to go before our line-in-the-sand date, we looked deeply at our finances and developed a budget that worked for us. We had some minimum criteria around our accommodation and transit requirements which somewhat affected our budget. These criteria included requirements that

Our nightly accommodation included a good kitchen

We sleep in a queen bed or bigger

Living rooms had furniture more comfortable than Ikea couches

Showers had to be bigger than us

We could walk to grocery or markets

No overnight transit unless it was long-distance flights

Our accommodation must have a washing machine for laundry.

Our Draft Budget

We drafted a budget of $4000 monthly where we each contributed $2000, making an annual budget of $48000. Roughly, we allocated $2000 to housing, $500 to wellness (including insurance, fitness, doctors), and $1000 to food and entertainment and $500 to transit. Because some countries are cheaper than others, our monthly expenses are fewer, so we focus on our annual budget and use the monthly as a guideline. Generally, in the months where we housesit, we spend more on transit and food. Months where we pay for housing, we eat in and cook more.

Telling the Family

With our dates set and budget outlined, the adventure didn't become real until we set out to tell our family. Telling our family about our travels was pretty straight forward. We're very lucky with our family network. Our families have always lived apart by several states or hours, so adding a few more hours or countries didn't really faze any family members. Traveling by planes and trains to see each other is commonplace with us. What's the difference between a 3-hour flight and an 8-hour one? Nothing, really.

Our aging parents cheered us on, encouraging us to enjoy our life to the fullest. Siblings just shrugged and smiled. All three of the kids, ages 17, 26, 31, enthusiastically supported us. Our youngest required a bit more conversation about her logistics in relation to college and where we'd domicile, but ultimately they were all thrilled for us. Their only request was they wanted to always know where we were and to have the option to visit. Here's the email we sent to the kids, and notice it included a request to them.

Dear ***

We are excited to share with you our plans that will launch in September 2021. At that time, we will head out on a worldwide journey for two years. Our plans will probably change, but for now we anticipate starting in Costa Rica, heading south through South America, to Australia, New Zealand, South Africa, Egypt, Israel, countries of Europe, and ending in Portugal.

Between now and September 2021, we plan to liquidate our possessions, down to one carry-on and one backpack each. Although we don't plan to maintain a storage unit, we realize we might need to have a small one. In the meantime, this means we've got to get rid of a lot of stuff, and sell our house.

So, we invite you to our house to go shopping! We will be selecting some items for each of you of things we each feel you individually should have. Things like heirlooms, family items, etc. that we will pick out just for each of you, and we would love for you to have them. The rest of the stuff in the house is up for grabs. And we mean everything!

Furniture, TVs, kitchen stuff, books, rugs, linens, beds, towels, art, camping gear, tools, sports gear, jewelry, etc. What you all don't take will go in an estate sale to the highest bidder....so please, don't be shy. Take what you want.

Timing is everything. Ideally, we'd like you to claim what you want by spring of 2021. Ideally, you could all be here at the same time, around spring time next year, so we're giving you a year to plan ahead. You are certainly invited to come earlier.

Please let us know if you have questions, and let's talk soon about timing.

We love all of you so much and can't wait to share the world with you,

Steve and Chris

Ultimately, the kids came to the house and scooped up many of our things. As our precious art and heirlooms left the house, I cried and cried. It was just stuff, but it was a lifetime of stuff. Eventually, though, I realized that with each item's departure, we were closer to our own get-away.

With most of the important heirlooms safely rehomed, we worked on getting our affairs in order. While the kids were at the house, we engaged in next-of-kin conversations and end-of-life scenarios. It wasn't fun, but it was necessary.

Getting Our Affairs in Order

Having been a single parent of a minor child, I already had wills and executors established. A quick update with my attorney since my child had reached adulthood was all I needed. But Steve had to start fresh on wills, powers of attorney, and health directives. The most difficult part of the entire process was trying to decide who would be in charge if we both died. This took lots of conversation and soul searching. It also took us a good six months to decide, so be sure to plan lots of time for this step.

Once we had our budget, told our family, and settled our affairs, we were ready for the disposal stage of our departure.

The Disposal Stage

In order to get rid of all of our stuff, we had to understand what stuff we had to get rid of. We began to think of the end—walking out of the house with two carry-ons and two backpacks—and developed a plan with the end in mind.

How Will We Carry Our Stuff?

We worked on the first question first, and getting that answer supplied the second question's answer too. We knew that no matter where we would go, we wanted to travel lightly. We had always been light travelers, and we saw no reason to change this style. Since we'd be carrying everything we owned, we didn't want to check baggage and fear losing it, nor did we want to pay baggage fees over and over again. In our carry-ons would go our assortment of shoes and clothes, and into our backpacks would go our tech gear, medicines, office supplies, and odds and ends.

There are many luggage choices out there, including backpacks,wheeled backpacks, and wheeled luggage. After using all the combinations on our various trips, including the around-the-world in 30 days trip, we've determined that the best combo of luggage for us is a wheeled carry-on bag and a day pack.

We went luggage shopping. I settled on what has become my favorite bag, the Eagle Creek Load Warrior. With lots of pockets in all the right places, durable corners and reliable wheels, this wunderkind expands if necessary (but don't pack it too full!) Its soft sides allow for it to get squeezed into hard-to-fit places, being far superior to the popular rigid, hard-sided luggage sold worldwide. Additionally, it's 22" and qualifies for all airlines' carry-on requirements.

Steve uses the Timbuk2 Co-Pilot and loves it for the same reasons. It has backpack straps, but Steve has yet to use them. It also has a lifetime warranty. With the amount of stress we put our luggage through, a lifetime warranty is a bonus.

For our backpacks, we aren't as particular, and we each love the ones we have. I have a Patagonia Chacabuco 30 DayPack, and Steve has the REI Co-op Trail 40 pack.

A Packing List

We packed for 72 degrees. We knew that if we needed warmer clothing for colder weather, we could stop in the various thrift and charity shops around the world to supplement for the short term. We're casual people who wear sporty activewear. We don't dress up much. We prefer a taco stand over a fine dining experience. We do laundry once a week. Our packing lists are roughly the same (click on each item to see the actual product I use):

- Four pairs of shorts
- Two skirt/skorts (use my referral code BIBCE275)
- Two pair of pants (no jeans)
- Six shirts
- Two work-out outfits (including black yoga pants)

- Seven pairs of underwear
- Three bras (one for workouts)
- Two pairs of socks (Bombas only!)
- One bathing suit
- Flat strappy sandals
- Athletic shoes that can be used to hike
- Everyday walking shoes for 10000 steps or more (my shoes)
- One hat for ponytails with wide brim (I love this hat!)
- A rain jacket/windbreaker

A Special Note about Shoes

Selecting shoes for our nomad life might have been one of the most difficult decisions we had to make. Since space was at a premium, bulky and heavy shoes were out. I cried when I got rid of my hiking boots, but I had to consider the costs/per wear ratios of every pair of shoes I carried.

Hiking boot ratio	super heavy:wear once a month.
Sandal ratio	very light:wear three times a month.
Athletic shoes ratio	moderate weight:wear three times a week
Everyday sandals ratio	moderate weight:wear every day

I narrowed seven pairs of shoes down to three: athletic shoes, everyday sandals, and strappy sandals. The everyday sandals are the Jeep of my shoe collection. Waterproof, durable, reliable, and they can go everywhere, including on beaches, trails, streets, ice (with socks!), planes, and deserts.

What's in the Backpacks?

Our backpacks do double duty. Not only do they carry the items below, but we also use them for day trips, overnights, and even grocery shopping. In our backpacks we pack the following items:

- Passports and paperwork
- Credit cards
- Cash
- Phone (I use a Pixel)
- Laptop (I love my Dell 13")
- Kindle (Can't beat a Paperwhite)
- Power cords
- Lip balm
- Medicines
- Lotions
- Toothbrush and toothpaste
- Earphones
- Small canvas tote
- Padlock
- Rubix cube
- Sewing kit
- First aid kit
- Small stapler
- Extra passport photos
- Tape
- Pen
- Notebook
- Filtering straw (Clean sip)

Once we knew what we'd take with us, we also knew what we didn't need. Everything we didn't need became everything we needed to get rid of. Overwhelmed, we were, but we dug in.

We took physical and emotional inventory of all the things in our house and our house itself. How would we sell it? What would we do with all of our stuff that we weren't taking with us? Where would we "live" for tax purposes? Would we need a safe deposit box? If so, where would it be?

Although we had preliminarily made the decision back in the cabin in the woods to sell the house, now we actually sat down and not only did the finances, we did a complete gut check around getting rid of the house.

Should We Sell the House?

With a 4 bedroom/3.5 bath in a high-end suburb of Denver, we knew we had to at least downsize. We had a house that we no longer needed, but we also knew that if we kept it, it would generate about $3500 in rent (not including expenses.) In addition, we had emotional attachments to the house; it was the place our youngest daughter would come "home" as she enjoyed her college breaks and summers. Would we be able to deal with the guilt of not having a "home for the holidays" for all our family members?

We went back and forth on the decision. When the market started to heat up, we thought about selling right then and there. But then where would we go in the short-term? We debated rental income versus investment income. Our answers were mixed. We could argue both ways. Some days we wanted to keep the house, and other days we couldn't wait to sell it. Our financial planner highlighted the financial pros and cons of all choices.

Finally, it came down to one simple question. Having been landlords before, did we want to be landlords again?

No.

We wanted freedom and flexibility. Owning a home would limit our ability to roam. So we finalized our plan to sell.

We also decided to work with our financial planner to put the money from the sale work generating revenue from the capital. In the future, if and when we buy our next residence, we'll have a bucket of money to spend on the next place we put down roots.

Should We Rent a Storage Unit?

We also reconsidered our decision not to rent a storage unit. After thinking it through, we reached the same conclusion we had about the house. We didn't want to be tied down. Keeping a storage unit was out.

This might have been the hardest decision yet; what would we do with all of our heirlooms and pictures that our kids didn't want? Finally, Steve and I had a heart to heart with each other. If we didn't get rid of the stuff now, our kids would have to deal with it all after we died. That's a burden that no one enjoys. Even though they were not at a perfect time in their lives to take our things, we reasoned there never would be a perfect time. We decided to proactively dispose of our things so that our kids wouldn't have to do it later.

The Timeline Starts Ticking

Now that the big decisions of house, stuff, and storage unit were finalized, we started working on the timeline to departure, including the loopholes of picking and domiciling in another state.

One Year Before Departure

A year before departure, we filled out a calendar with the things we had to do over the coming year. We took inventory of everything we would use in the next year, organized it into categories, and made plans for each category. The categories were: The Good Stuff, The Estate Sale/Garage Sale Stuff, The Special Handling Stuff, The Last Minute Stuff, and Trash. Each category got its own action plan and timeline for disposal, starting with the Good Stuff.

Getting Rid of the Good Stuff

With the timeline in hand, I struggled with the decisions about how we would dispose of the "good stuff," including my favorite artwork. We invited the kids to the house to take the Good Stuff. Before the kids came to the house, Steve and I each made piles of a few things we wanted different people, including our children and our own siblings, to have. These items included some heirloom and genealogical things and particular pieces of jewelry and ephemeral. When the kids arrived, we told them that we wanted them to have these items in particular. If they didn't want them, that was okay, but *they* had to throw them out when they left.

It was tough on them and us. The kids were hesitant at first. It was weird for them to go through their parents' stuff and just take things. We had to convince them to act as if we were dead. Would they rather come and take

41

things while we were alive or come later and have to sort through things when we were dead? "Becoming dead" allowed us to emotionally detach from items and get into disposal mode.

The kids took most of the good things. Art, vases, jewelry, some collectibles, a few household items, and one of the TVs. Although these items could fetch good money at an estate sale, the challenge with art, especially, is finding the right buyer who wants to pay the value of the piece.

For us, we'd rather give these items to our kids for them to enjoy (and for us to enjoy when we visit) than try to find picky buyers who would demand provenance and appraisals. Besides, we knew that the Good Stuff that the kids didn't want would draw good buyers to our pending estate sale.

Ultimately, I had to cry a few pieces away. Focusing on our retirement vision helped me dispose of things. Sometimes I just had to eat some chocolate. The process was painful but freeing. Steve struggled with rehoming heirlooms that we had inherited. Although he passed them on to his children, it felt like a coming of age moment for him, and one he wasn't quite ready to do. But he did.

After we handed over the heirlooms and artwork, there were many things that the kids didn't want, including the photo albums, china, and most of the furniture. These items moved into either the Estate/Garage Sale Category or the Special Handling Category. With the remaining items, our goal was to get the most money we could get for our stuff with the fewest number of personal interactions. We didn't want to deal with buyer after buyer, if they even showed up, nickel and dime-ing each transaction.

Six Months Before Departure

With the Good Stuff gone, we focused on the items we would sell in the estate sale/garage sale.

Planning for the "Estate Sale/Garage Sale" Stuff

With the majority of The Good Stuff gone to the kids, we had to decide how we wanted to get rid of the next category, Estate Sale/Garage Sale stuff. For us, we just wanted to get rid of it. We didn't care how much money we got for these remaining items. Our goal was to clean out the house and make sure it was empty and ready for us to sell it.

Selling through Garage Sales, Craigslist, Marketplace?

We debated many ways to sell off the Estate Sale/Garage Sale stuff, including the dreaded yard sales, craigslist, and Facebook marketplace listings. We knew we'd never get what we paid for on any of our things. Plus, if we were already financially situated, would another $100 in our pockets really make a difference? We had to release our *emotional* attachment to our stuff–like Steve's owl collection and my wedding China–in order to make decisions on getting rid of all of it.

We choose not to hassle with direct-to-consumer options. Often the buyers that come to your house through these classifieds are picky, cheap, and unreliable. Yes, there are exceptions and we've sold a few things successfully through these venues. But in general, because we had an entire household of goods which could be sold to hundreds of different buyers with varying levels of tastes and budgets, we chose to use an estate seller.

Steve was still working, so I took on this part of the disposal. I didn't want to negotiate every sale, and I didn't want to watch my life-long possessions leave the house over and over. It was too hard emotionally. I made calls to various estate sellers, ultimately picking one that had a national and regional scope. I liked that they had several websites to draw people to our house, appealing to outdoor enthusiasts, art lovers, antique dealers, and furniture buyers.

Using an Estate Seller

Repeatedly, the estate seller told me not to dispose of *anything*. They said that they could sell everything in our house. Whatever they didn't sell, they offered to find a junk hauler to take the rest for an additional fee. We didn't want to pay for them to dispose of whatever remained. We came up with a different plan involving a free-for-all open house. Keep reading.

Giving Things Away

We knew that after the estate sale, we'd still have things left in the house that we'd have to get rid of prior to showing the house. This was the unexpected "Trash" Category. We reserved a U-haul for the day after the estate sale, and we figured that whatever didn't sell, we'd load up and take to a charity shop. We also scheduled the estate sale for the weekend before our city's "big trash" pick up day. This is the one day of the month that the city allows for extra-large items in our trash. We figured the city would take most of what was left, and we'd cancel the U-haul at the last minute if necessary.

Three-Six Before Departure

While we waited for the estate sale, we worked on the Special Handling category. We found a few items that we felt we could either sell ourselves or that deserved better homes than with those folks who would show up at the estate sale. We wanted our stuff to go to people who really needed it or wanted it. We sorted through these items and came up with particular plans.

Yearbooks

My personal rule of thumb is don't spend time looking at stuff that is tough to dispose of. You'll lose your momentum and the gumption to get rid of things. (If you have a box of stuff in the basement you haven't looked at in years, don't open it!) But, alas, I got sucked into my yearbooks, and this is what happened.

Fortunately, I am a member of a Facebook group from the community where I went to middle school and junior high, and in that group are several friends with whom I maintain a connection. As I was going through the yearbooks, I found the places where old school mates had signed my book. I posted a few of their messages to the Facebook group, and this action drew lots of comments from the collective class. This got the attention of the local library who then reached out and asked if they could have the yearbooks.

The next day I mailed them off. It cost me $3.33 via media mail and now the yearbooks are not only in a place I could see them again if I ever get the hankering, but they'll also benefit many other people. It's a win-win. I did this for my high school yearbooks as well.

Photo Albums and Photos

Whereas disposing of the yearbooks was easy, disposing of the photo albums was not. Ultimately, Steve and I scanned all the pages/photos within the albums and put them into Google Photos. Because I have a Pixel phone, I get unlimited storage. We also moved all my other digital photos that are on drives and phones into this Photos account and gave our youngest daughter access to the account. She then perused all the hard-copy albums, snagging prints that she felt she wanted to keep in her keepsake box. When this process finished, we dumped every album into the garbage on a Sunday night. Early on Monday morning, the garbage team picked them up, and they're now gone. There was no time to change our minds, hard as it was. Whereas I thought my daughter would want the wedding photo album of her dad and me, she did not.

China and Glassware

I inherited a complete set of Noritake china and all of my Grandma's Depression Glass serving pieces along with the silver serving spoons and silver serving utensils. I gave the silver and a few of the Depression Glass items, which I shipped via Amtrak, to my sister across the country. As for the remaining China pieces, no one in the family wanted them. None of the China resale places wanted them, nor did Goodwill. Consignment shops didn't want them either. I even called pawn shops to see if they'd buy them for the gold on the rims. I asked *everywhere*. No one, including our kids, wanted these antique glassware and pieces. Thus, they were part of the estate sale and sold for pennies.

Plants

I gave all our plants away to folks in my local gardening club. I posted on Facebook that I had potted plants to give to new homes, put them on my porch, and people came and grabbed them. I also offered a day for them to collect seeds from my cherished native garden in my yard.

Paints, Toxic Chemicals, Fertilizer, Compacts Discs, Computers

After going through the garage and under the sinks, we found buckets of hazardous items we couldn't throw away in the garbage or sell in the estate sale. We found a hazmat place that would take the items, and we paid a per-pound price for their removal. Our local city waste department allowed for a couple of computers and some larger batteries. The rest went to the hazmat company.

As for smaller batteries, Target and Best Buy took our used batteries and cell phones.

Pets

The sad truth is that it's very difficult to travel with pets. Many people do. We had a Giant Schnauzer named Zeus. Deciding what to do with him was a very difficult decision. We even looked into traveling with him, but due to his size, it was impossible. He was too big for the largest PETA-approved carrier. Not only could we not fly with him, he was too big for the QE2, a cruise ship that allows pets. It took quite some time for us to decide what to do with him.

Thankfully, a loving family member begged to take him. We knew that she would adopt him into her home, and we could see him on visits when we returned to the States. My girlfriend and I drove him across the country to deliver him to his new home safely. I cried almost the entire way.

Housesitting helps fill the hole left by not having our dog with us.

Mattresses

One of our biggest concerns was our king-sized Theperpaedic mattress that weighed at least 100 pounds. Of course, it was upstairs in the master bedroom which was furthest from the street. We fretted over how we'd dispose of this monster. Charities typically won't take them; they must be sold or thrown away. We even reserved a U-haul so that we could haul it to the dump in case our garbage team didn't take it. Luckily, it sold in the estate sale, which we didn't expect. Our twin and queen mattress also sold.

Clothing

Steve and I were surprised at how attached we were to our favorite pieces of clothing, especially the lounge-around-the-house hoodies and sweats. Steve had a lifetime career of suits and neckties; none of which had been worn in the years of Covid. It was easy for him to let them go. I had an entire collection of hiking clothes that I had spent lots of money on and I felt represented me. They were my identity. They all had to go so I gathered all my girlfriends for a hike then sold them my hiking wardrobe, hiking backpacks, hiking hats, hiking boots, and other hiking paraphernalia. Occasionally, when they all get together, they'll send me a picture of them wearing my stuff. The rest of our clothes, including my wedding dress, went in the estate sale.

One Month Before Departure

By the time we approached our last month, the house was barely functional. The estate company came and priced all the things that would go in the estate sale. We had packed all of our things we were taking with us and locked them in a closet to hide them away. The only three categories that remained were The Estate Sale/Garage Sale Stuff, Last Minute Stuff, and Stuff that Didn't

Sell. A few Special Handling things remained and were moved into our Last Minute Stuff category.

Meanwhile, Steve and I were on auto pilot. We crossed things off our lists rapidly, talked through logistics on a daily basis, and anxiously anticipated our departure date. We had a few things we really wanted to do before leaving Denver; go to one last Red Rocks concert, hike in our beloved mountains, eat at our favorite vegan restaurants, and emotionally say good-bye to a place we loved. Neither of us had moved away from a place that we loved before. At times, we wondered why we were messing with our well-ordered lives.

As for our work lives, I sold off my DenverByFoot brand, transferred all my social media handles for my Denver life, and said good-bye to my Denver hiking persona. Steve made the phone call he had been dreading for six months. Even though he was beyond thrilled to retire, thinking about making the call cost him many sleepless nights. His responsible, employee psyche asked how he could quit a job where he'd gotten Rookie of the Year? How could he let his team down by quitting? How could he look his boss in the eye and quit after just 18 months? Finally, he made the call. Fortunately, he and his boss agreed to the terms of his final days. Once he hung up, Steve finally felt he was ready to go.

With four weeks to go before departure, pressure mounted to get it all done. We ate through our pantry, notified companies of our change of address, and had our last lunches and cuppas with friends. Real estate agents started to hear that our house would be up for sale, and we quietly showed the house even before officially listing it. Although our plan had been to sell the house empty after the estate sale, we accepted an offer on the house and its appliances by a buyer, sight unseen and $75,000 over our asking price. We never had to list our house. In the last few weeks before departure, we worked on the things required for escrow, and got rid of the Last Minute Items, our bikes and the car.

Bikes

Since we wanted to ride bikes up to the day before we left town, we held on to them until the last minute, and they sold in 20 minutes via a Facebook post. We threw in the bike helmets, shoes, locks, and pumps with the sale because we didn't need them anymore. The new owners were thrilled.

Car

Since we were planning a long road trip and departing the country via the Newark airport, we kept our car for a little longer. We drove it to see all of our friends and family, then we sold it via Carvana, the car company, at our departure city. They made an offer we couldn't refuse. They picked up the car at the hotel the night before we flew out and deposited the money in our bank account the same day. We took the hotel's shuttle to the airport.

The Things that Didn't Sell

After our estate sale, there were still a few items lying around the house. These items become the Things that Didn't Sell Category. Rather than packing them all up and taking them to Goodwill (or other), we decided to have a "Free for All" open house. On the day before the extra trash pick-up day, we posted on Facebook Marketplace the following listing:

Everything is FREE.
Preference in first hour to teachers, non-profits
and those collecting for homelessness.

12-4.

Must take immediately.

Kitchen stuff

Linens

Tents

Sleeping bags

Office supplies

Clarinet

Jewelry

Women's clothes sizes 4-12

Men's clothing size M-L, 34

Winter jackets, gloves, hats. Adult sizes

Small kitchen appliances

Suitcases

Pots and pans

Makeup

Home decor

Overstuffed chair

Sporting goods

ALL FREE

At 11:30, the line started. It was 30 deep by 12:00. In the rain! We let 5 people in at a time, giving them 10 minutes to scour the house. Within 45 minutes, we had 5% left of all of our stuff. By 3:45, everything was gone. Every piece of furniture, clothing, linen…everything. Seriously, the only thing left was trash. We bagged up six bags of trash, put them on the street for "Big Trash" pick up, and canceled the UHaul we thought we'd need to take the remainders for donation. By the time the city came by the next morning to get our weekly trash, only one bag of trash remained for pick up. One.

Thus, we got rid of everything in our house without a single trip to the dump, a thrift store, or a church.

By this point, I was exhausted emotionally. Once all our stuff started leaving the house, it was easier. But by the end of the weekend when we had our estate sale, our Free for All open house, and our extra garbage day, I broke down in tears. What had we done? Steve hugged me.

Our Actual Real-Life Timeline of Disposal

Here is our actual timeline. Starting with the first idea of becoming nomads to the day we left the country, we stepped through the process on or around the following dates.

2009	Discussed the idea to be nomads
May 2018	Batted around slow travel nomad ideas
October 2019	Designed our full-time traveling nomad lifestyle
May 25, 2020	Set a line in the sand for our departure date
Sept 7, 2020	Developed possible itinerary
Oct 1, 2020	Notified family of our plans
Dec 25, 2020	Last holidays together "in old life"
March 15, 2021	Took dog to family friend for permanent residency
April 1, 2021	Kids came and took whatever they wanted
April 15, 2021	Took first trip to Texas to establish domicile
April 15, 2021	Began domiciling in Texas

April 16, 2021 deposit box	Deposited jewelry and paperwork in Texas safe
April 20, 2021	Began dispersing stuff to friends and charities
May 23, 2021	Listed house unofficially
May 23, 2021	Accepted offer on house
May 25, 2021	Goodbye party with friends
May 26, 2021	Sold bikes
May 27, 2021	Estate sale for three days
May 30, 2021	"Free for All" Open House
May 31, 2021	Big Trash Pick Up Day
June 2, 2021	Departed Denver for road trip
June 30, 2021	Closed on house & turned off utilities
July 3, 2021	Finished domiciling paperwork in Texas
July 5, 2021	Sold car
July 6, 2021	Boarded plane for Ireland

The Leaving Stage

With all our stuff sorted and our itinerary booked, we started working on the Leaving Stage. This stage overlapped with the Disposal Stage. While talking through all our questions about selling the house and deciding where to get a safe deposit box, we worked through the questions about where we would "live." What started as the question, "Where will we get our mail?" we eventually learned about the concepts of domiciling and residency. With no home to have an address, we could pick any state we wanted. Plus, with our youngest daughter making the decision to go to college out of the country, we didn't have to think about in-state college tuition.

We figured we had 50 choices. We narrowed them down to the state-income-tax free states of Wyoming, Washington, Texas, South Dakota, Nevada, Florida, and Alaska. From that list, we narrowed it down to Florida and Texas simply based on the fact that we knew we never wanted to live in the snow again.

Domiciling (Or Where We Get Our Mail)

After talking with several lawyers and accountants who implored us to pick a state where we would likely live, we picked Texas. They advised us that our previous state, Colorado, might come after us for back taxes if Colorado didn't believe our story that we lived in Texas. Our lawyers encouraged us to not only establish our domicile and residency, but to also become part of the community. We should join a social club, get a library card, register to vote, volunteer, and hire our professional services people in the city where we'd domicile.

Some friends turned us on to Livingston, Texas, a tiny town north of Houston, where there is a company named RV Escapees. They cater to the thousands of full-time RVers who travel the US and have the same problem as us. Many full-time RVers also do not have a home to place a mailbox nor an address. RV Escapees has figured out how to help people establish their residency, offer a mail service, assist with voting, and even provide professional services. We reviewed their benefits and costs and signed up.

Getting all the paperwork figured out took two trips to Texas. During our first trip, we signed up with RV Escapees where we received our own Texas mailing address. We also secured a safe deposit box where we placed jewelry and paper work so that we didn't have to worry about these items during our estate sale. Once we had our mailing address, we changed our address of record with our banks two months ahead of our move so that we would have two months of statements with our new Texas address. We needed these statements to prove a local address to the DMV.

Two months later when we actually had sold and left our house in Colorado, we returned to Texas. On this trip, we took our bank statements with our new address to the Texas drivers license office and used these items as our proof of residency. Those statements together with our social security cards and Colorado drivers license were the items we needed to get a Texas drivers license. We surrendered our Colorado drivers licenses, and with our new licenses, we registered to vote.

Finally, with our new documents in place, we could claim domicile and residency in Texas, and ultimately leave the country. Now when we travel, we say we live in Texas, and we tell people that if and when we return to the US, we will live in Texas. Whether we will ever live in the US again, we have no idea. But if we do return to the US, we'll return to Texas, and from there, we'll start our next plan.

Medical Insurance, Travel Insurance, and Liability Insurance as Nomads

This section is for US citizens. It doesn't apply, except maybe conceptually, to anyone else in the world. In addition, we are younger than 65 years old, so the US Medicare system doesn't apply to us.

With no medical insurance once Steve left his job, we had to figure out what to do for medical coverage while traveling the world. Even though we had had good experiences with out-of-pocket care on previous world trips, we still wanted to carry some type of coverage as we traveled.

We researched our medical health insurance options, and we weeded through the clutter and the noise to determine the best health insurance option for us.

Sorting through the Different Types of Insurance

When we started this process of finding insurance, it was very unclear to us exactly what we needed and how to get it. We were looking for insurance that would cover our ongoing medical needs while we traveled as nomads. Once we left the US, we would not have any medical insurance that covered us in the US. So we sorted, researched, and asked a lot of questions. Things became clear once we understood the different terms. We break them down here:

Travel Insurance

This type of insurance covers you for the times when the travel gods are not in your favor. Think lost luggage, canceled flights, missed connections. If something bad happens, your travel insurance will reimburse you in a variety of ways for missed flights, botched hotel reservations, etc.

Most good travel credit cards have this type of coverage as a benefit and it's automatically included if you book your trip with said credit card. The Chase Sapphire Preferred is an excellent card that includes Travel Insurance. Read the fine print; you may be able to skip buying a stand-alone Travel Insurance policy if your credit card covers such items.

Travel Insurance with Medical

This type of insurance includes all the coverage mentioned above for Travel Insurance, and it also includes dramatic stuff like getting hit by a bus, needing evacuation due to terrorism, or food poisoning. The underlying assumption to most of these types of policies is that you have insurance at home and that you will transport yourself back to the US to finish your medical care under your current medical insurance in the US.

Many good travel credit cards (such as the Chase Sapphire Preferred mentioned above) include this type of coverage. You may be able to skip buying a stand-alone Travel Insurance with Medical policy if your credit card covers such items. Sadly, many policies, including credit card policies, do not cover COVID scenarios. Read your fine print. You may have to buy a COVID policy, not only for your protection, but because some countries require proof of COVID coverage before entering.

We have a whole suite of Chase cards and either book with our Chase cards or our American Express cards. Although Amex isn't well accepted throughout the world, it is widely accepted for booking travel. We decide between the two based on what types of travel point kickers the cards have at the time of purchase. Both Chase and Amex, depending on the card, give great travel insurance with medical.

Medical Insurance/Health Insurance/Global Medical Insurance

This is the type of insurance we're used to in the US. It covers catastrophic needs, chronic illnesses, acute medical scenarios, emergency room care, etc. Many people in the US have this type of coverage through their employer or they buy it through the Affordable Care Act Exchanges (Obamacare) or other.

This is the type of insurance that we needed and purchased and is not covered by our credit card benefits.

Nomad Insurance, Global Nomad, Expat Insurance:

You'll see terms like "nomad insurance", "global nomad insurance", or "expat insurance. "These are various terms, brands, and websites that target Americans who live abroad. These are the terms we often see to describe the type of insurance we need. But regardless of the terminology or branding used, it's all Global Medical/Health Insurance. What makes these terms confusing is that the brand names are actually brokers who sell Travel Insurance, Travel Insurance with Medical, and Global Medical Insurance. In addition, some brokers with brand names only sell Travel Insurance but make it look like it's Global Medical Insurance. (Safetywing, Allianz, and World Nomads are examples.)

Buying Medical Insurance

After reviewing lots of websites and sorting through all the options, we narrowed it down to a couple of likely companies. We still had questions, though, and discovered that in our experience, there was no price difference between going directly to the insurance provider's website or talking directly to a broker.

Brokers Differ Drastically: Here's Who We Used

We talked to two completely different brokers. Both of them represented the same sets of companies, but each had very different advice and understanding of the policies. Although they both recommended the same company to us, the price quoted between the two of them was drastically different.

The broker we decided to work with eloquently discussed the differences and also developed quotes for us that were cheaper than the first broker. We recommend:

Justin Barsketis justin.b@expatinsurance.com +1 435 647 6379.

He is also on WhatsApp, which is a super feature for when we travel internationally and don't want to pay international communication fees. Please tell him we sent you.

The Main Global Medical Insurance Providers

Although there are probably more providers than we'll mention here, the major US providers of global medical/health insurance for Americans are GeoBlue (Blue Cross/Blue Shield), Aetna, Cigna, and IMG. When we went through their quoting tools on our own, we got extremely different price quotes, varying by almost $2000 monthly.

We did our best to answer all the questions on the website equally so that we could compare apples to apples. We focused on our deductible and lifetime benefit amounts. When we scanned the differences in coverage between the cheapest and the most expensive providers, we found miniscule differences in the coverage.

We sorted through all the quotes and returned to our broker to confirm what we were reading. He could not explain why the relatively same policies would differ so much in price. We ran through our health scenarios and our risk tolerance, and he confirmed our choice and talked through our exclusions. Additionally, we sorted through reviews and looked specifically for comments about claims. No single company necessarily rose above another.

Medical Health Shares

After reviewing medical health share companies like Sedera and Liberty, we decided they were not a fit for us, particularly because they generally also included US coverage. We're not looking for US coverage.

Prescriptions

Prior to losing our insurance, we filled our prescriptions to the maximum amounts allowed by our insurance policy. Then, we asked our doctors to write prescriptions that would extend past the dates listed on our bottle labels. We took photos of these and put them on Google Drive. In addition, we use GoodRX.com to fill when our insurance doesn't apply. Finally, we've been successful buying drugs at local pharmacies globally where no prescriptions are needed. One example of this is Cipro!

Our Medical/Health Scenarios and Underwriting

We are both healthy with no chronic illnesses. Steve is 61, I am 55. I had a hysterectomy due to cervical cancer four years ago with no recurrence.

Our broker accurately stated that we would have to go through underwriting, and regardless of whom we'd choose, I would get an exclusion for my female parts until I had a clear medical record for five years. Conversely, I could pay almost 5x the monthly premium to have my uterus covered. And I thought, hum, why should I pay to have a part covered that I don't have anymore? (This is my risk tolerance, and not something I'm recommending for someone else.)

In underwriting, the provider kicked me out of "Silver" level down to Bronze. This limited my lifetime coverage from $5million to $1million and excluded my female parts. I can apply for Silver on the fifth anniversary of my surgery. For Steve, the underwriter asked for a copy of his medical records from his last wellness check, including the notes. They put him in the Silver category with one exclusion for a minor condition, and he has a $5000 deductible with $5million lifetime coverage.

What Insurance We Selected, How Much We Pay, What It Covers

Ultimately, we selected IMG Bronze for me and IMG Silver for Steve. We will pay about $175 a month with a $5000 annual deductible, a $1million lifetime coverage for me and a $5million lifetime coverage for Steve. We have set aside a $5000 annual medical fund of our own to cover dental, massages, out-of-pocket procedures and co-pays. Our policy does not include COVID-19 coverage (we are vaccinated for it), but it does include one annual wellness check and prescription coverage (with limits.) In addition, we purchased a Travel Policy with Medical for $200 annually that covers COVID and trip cancellation scenarios. We purchased this so we can freely roam in countries that require COVID coverage.

We were so worried about health care because it's so expensive and complicated in the US that we assumed it would be like that in other countries. So far, it's not.

As medical issues have come up while we travel, we've made appointments, paid out of pocket, and generally had better coverage of our medical needs than if we were in the US.

We'll need to be in the US at some time over our travels. At that time, we'll assess whether or not we're comfortable with our credit card travel benefit coverage or if we want to buy a Travel Insurance with Medical policy for a month or so. Granted our IMG coverage won't extend in the US, but we're willing to accept some risk for the short time periods we'll be in the US.

Doctors Visits Around the World

In the rest of the world, the price of medicine is reasonable. Here are five examples of care we've received while traveling.

Medical Example One: While traveling throughout South America, my knees started to give me trouble. By the time I got to Mexico, I was hobbling from bus stop to bus stop. A Spanish-speaking friend helped me make an appointment with a knee specialist.

On the day of the appointment, I arrived at ABC Hospital, the best hospital in Mexico City. I met my doctor only to find out that he had recently returned from Aspen. During the winter months, he practices medicine at the ski slopes in Colorado where he sees hundreds of middle-aged skiers who've cracked their knees. He's considered the best doctor in Colorado for knee work.

This orthopedic surgeon comes home to Mexico in the off-season to be with his family and continue practicing. At the consultation, he did complete x-rays and administered one cortisone shot in each knee. I left the office without pain and only $300 lighter in my wallet.

Estimated price in US without insurance: $2000

Medical Example Two: A few years later in the UK, my knee pain returned. I saw a doctor and got a cortisone shot while in Liverpool for $150. In addition, a visit to the chiropractor for a full evaluation and several adjustments cost $60.

Estimated price in US without insurance: $800

Medical Example Three: Pain returned to my knees. In Puerto Vallarta, I saw another specialist. He did x-rays, a complete MRI, and exam. I received a hyaluronic acid shot in my knee and five hours of physical therapy. Total cost was: $912.

Estimated price in US without insurance: $6000

Medical Example Four: Steve and I got our teeth cleaned for $30 each, and he got a tooth implant for $1200 in Mexico.

Estimated price in US without insurance: $3500

Medical Example Five: Again in Mexico, I got my annual wellness exam. The wellness exam, including mammography, ultrasound and pap smear cost $47.

Estimated price in US without insurance: $1200

I used to lead hiking adventures in Oaxaca, Mexico. On one of those adventures, a hiker fell and broke her femur. Evacuated by the Roja Cruz (Red Cross) for free, she had emergency surgery in Oaxaca where they placed 13 pins in her leg and knee. A week's stay with full-time nurses kept her

TWO CARRY-ONS AND A PLAN

comfortable in recovery until she could get home. The entire bill came to $9700 (which ultimately Kaiser Permanente insurance paid 80%.) In addition, another lady on the trip ended up with severe abdominal cramping. We visited the local walk-in clinic. She was seen for free and medicated for free by a doctor.

We tell you these stories to illustrate how medical care outside of the US is accessible, affordable, and in many cases, world class. With this information and experience, we decided to budget $5000 a year each for any out-of-pocket medical and wellness expenses while also carrying a global medical insurance policy to protect us from unexpected issues and catastrophic scenarios. This $5000 sits outside of our normal monthly budget, and we track it as its own line item. Thus, our annual budget is truly $48000 plus $5000 for out-of-pocket medical expenses. At the end of the year, we replenish the $5000 if necessary.

66

The Nomad Travel Stage

While we were getting rid of all of our stuff and establishing our insurance, we started thinking about the actual travel and nomad side of our life. Factoring in the opposite seasons across the hemispheres and our departure timeline, we figured our first, rough itinerary. We'd leave Denver and head to Costa Rica in September, hang out in Central America and northern South America for the fall (their spring) and winter (their summer), heading down through South America. We'd jump the ocean to Australia, pop over to New Zealand, jump up to South Africa, drop into the middle east, and finish up in western Europe.

I could see a horseshoe shape on our trip that spanned two years. At first, we felt that two years would be enough time to find a full-time place to live, but we soon realized that two years wasn't enough time to enjoy all the countries we wanted to visit. Rather than eliminate destinations or travel more quickly, we decided to toss out our two-year deadline.

By planning on Costa Rica as our first stop, we figured we could easily drop our daughter off at college and head south. We had a plan.
Then, we didn't.
It was our first lesson in flexibility. Our daughter threw us a curveball. She got accepted to Trinity College in Dublin. And she wanted us to drop her off.

Dublin was supposed to be the end of our trip, not the beginning! And to top it all off, our second test in flexibility arrived with COVID hitting the world's travel plans. We started to realize that we could only plan 4-6 weeks at a time.

With borders and COVID restrictions changing daily, we had to keep an eye on flexibility.

Here's the funny thing. All along, we had been keeping a faithful eye on the housesits that came up. After planning and researching housesitting as a strategy, we wanted to include it in our plans. But with Covid in full swing, all the housesits in the Americas closed. No one was traveling, and no one was listing their house in Costa Rica nor anywhere else. Surprisingly lots of folks were listing their houses in the UK.

Maybe going to Dublin and then over to the UK wouldn't be so bad after all? We began making our first sets of reservations, and we developed a system around "anchors." Anchors might be fabulous places we want to stay, amazing housesits, interesting things we want to do, or particular people we want to see. We then develop our travel plans around those anchors.

Dublin would be our first anchor followed by any anchors we could plant in the UK. We would visit one of the world's most expensive countries affordably by taking housesits all over the UK. We would be able to see Rochester, Canterbury, Kent, London, Liverpool, Glasgow and Bristol via the housesitting community. First we'd visit Dublin and drop our daughter off, enjoy Ireland a bit, then scoot across the Irish Sea for some time in the UK. It'd be late summer/early fall. Although the temperature might be a bit chillier than 72 degrees, we'd be just fine.

We booked our long-leg flights to Dublin. With our departure date and location firm, we then set our dates to sell it all and move forward.

What is long-leg travel? We think of it as those airline trips that cross big bodies of water and go over multiple countries. We try to "save up" for these types of travel trips, and we pay for them with our rewards points on various airlines or credit cards. But sometimes, the rate will be so good, we go ahead and pay cash. Our trip from Newark to Dublin was only $300. We paid cash for that; otherwise, it would have "cost" several thousand mileage points. The cash price was better than the points price in comparison.

Our Nightly Accommodations

Each night, we must pay for housing. Because of our comfort criteria, we find that Airbnb most often meets our requirements. But when we plan, we generally start by looking for housesits first. Housesitting is a huge part of our nomad strategy. Whenever we think about our next anchor, we think about getting a housesit there, first. We set up travel alerts in the Trusted Housesitters app to get us tuned into what's happening with housesitting in a particular location. We dream a bit too. We think about where we would ideally like to be (in the city center with a cat), and then we allow for our boundaries. Whereas we might take a housesit outside of the city center with a dog, we most likely won't take one out in the country with a melee of fur.

If there's a particular place we really want to go, we'll look at paying for a location to stay. If we really want to be in Rome in April, we might wait a bit to see if a housesit shows up. But the longer we wait on a housesit, the fewer the accommodation options will be. It's a tricky balance like the scales of justice! If we book a housesit too early, we might miss out on the perfect housesit. If we book one too late, we might miss out on the perfect Airbnb.

As for how Steve and I divy up the work of our logistics life, we're still finding our own niches within our relationship. I track the housesits, while Steve is really good at finding Airbnbs. Together we play the air travel roulette games, each researching flights and watching for fare trends. We try to limit all of our travel and logistics talk to Tuesdays so that we aren't consumed by it daily. Since we have no end to our travel in sight, the logistics can get overwhelming.

Housesitting and Why Do We Do It

We love pets, especially dogs. As nomads, we can't have pets, and we miss our Giant Schnauzer, Zeus, greatly. In addition, as part of our overall plan to travel, we're in the most expensive cities and areas in the world. Trying to fit those expensive locations into our budget is tough. So, we look to housesitting as a strategy that satisfies both needs: a love for pets and a love for budget travel.

There are many ways to housesit. Some people professionally housesit, charging for their services as they move about the world. Since we are not interested in receiving revenue, we housesit around the philosophy of a mutual exchange of services. The homeowners get a trusted couple to take care of their home and pets, and we, in return, get a nice place to stay and the pet cuddles we sorely miss.

We find each other through a website called Trusted Housesitters. This website vets all its users, has a robust review community, and even allows users to buy liability insurance. We have been members for almost three years because we started housesitting before we even left our home. Why? It's part of our housesitting strategy.

Our Housesitting Strategy

Within the Trusted Housesitters community, there are "good" housesits and "bad" housesits. Determining the difference between the two might be subjective, but for us, we find "good" housesits to be fewer than two dogs or cats, great locations, use of a car, great wifi, and walkable to great sites. A "bad" housesit, for example, might be ten cats, all requiring medication, and located down a dirt road away from everything.

Good housesits can be quite competitive to find. Paris under the Eiffel Tower, anyone? So, in order to be competitive, you have to be highly reviewed and readily available. But how do you get highly reviewed if you haven't had your first housesit?

Knowing that we'd want to housesit in good and competitive locations, we started locally in Denver before we even left town. We took anything that came our way. An overnight with three dogs on medications? Took it. On a farm with llamas? Took it. A thread-bare flat with a greyhound? Soon, we had a five-star portfolio of a variety of animals and situations. When we started applying to overseas housesits, we got them.

How We Pick A Housesit

Housesitting is work. It changes the tone of our stay in a community. It has its rewards, and it has its limitations, too. So we chose to do housesits in a location when the following conditions are in place:

1. The price of a month's accommodation exceeds our monthly housing budget of $2000. Generally, we housesit in the more expensive countries and use Airbnb in less expensive countries

71

2.   When the location of the housesit can't be beat. Homeowners often offer up gorgeous properties that we would never be able to afford otherwise. We've stayed in downtown London penthouses, in large ocean front properties, and even deep in jungles. It was worth the experience and luxury of the homes to give up some freedom and flexibility.

3.   When the pets' schedules are easy and allow for great movement and exploration. *Generally*, when housesitting for dogs, you'll have 4-6 hours a day to explore. With cats and caged animals, you can leave the home for longer periods. Sometimes, there are no pets and the homeowner just wants someone at the home in the evenings and nights.

Be Flexible and Recalculate Constantly

We started accepting housesits all over the UK. And suddenly, our itinerary took shape. We headed to Dublin first and then spent six weeks in the UK.

While in the UK, we started working on our next move. We were so close to Europe, why not continue our fun in Europe for the fall into the winter? We kept looping back to our goal of staying in 72 degrees and came upon our first itinerary challenge. There's no place in Europe that is regularly 72 degrees throughout the winter.

We kept looking at weather histories for Greece and the southern Mediterranean countries, but nothing suited our needs. Closer by, we started reviewing the southeast Asia countries. Sadly, with COVID raging everywhere and travel being completely unpredictable, Thailand, Japan, Korea, the Philippines, Vietnam and other Pacific countries had closed their doors. We determined that those countries which closed first to American travelers would also be the last ones to open.

Managing the Unexpected

When we first started our travels, COVID was all the rage. The world's countries closed up, our choices of where to go narrowed. While we didn't want to plan too far ahead, we had to plan a bit ahead in order to either find housesits before others did, or find Airbnbs before they sold out.

It was a balancing act tempered by the world's health and its politics. Finally, we realized that Mexico in the winter would fit all of our needs and it would also likely be the last country to close to Americans due to a resurgence of Covid. But it felt "wrong" to fly back over the pond when we had only just left it. Mexico wasn't even in our original plans!

In order to cope with the constantly changing Covid rules, we tracked the latest news at the individual country's websites about Covid and made sure that any reservations we made accommodated for Covid cancellations. In addition, we added Travel Insurance to our insurance portfolio to cover us for Covid cancellations. We stopped saying " We plan to.." and replaced it with "We're flexing to…"

But whether its Covid, geopolitical infighting, or changes to airline schedules, change is a given. Thus, we watch the daily headlines and build flexibility into our plans. We wait as long as possible to secure housesits, and we make sure we have a few days of flexibility on both ends of the housesits to accommodate for last-minute changes in flights and/or Covid requirements.

We also make sure that we can get tested near airports in a timely fashion to the countries' requirements where we are traveling through, to and from.

Two Housesits and Airbnb Examples in Real Life

On our visit to the UK, including Ireland and Northern Ireland, we mixed a combo of Airbnb and housesits in order to achieve several goals. At our first stop in Dublin, we wanted to have a place that would comfortably work for Steve and me plus our daughter who we were dropping off at college. Not knowing if a housesit would come up that would meet three pieces of criteria (location, size, and Steve, me and our daughter), we went ahead and paid for an Airbnb. Fortunately for us, the owner of the home threw in her car for us to use, reducing our overall expenses and allowing us great flexibility for all the things we wanted to do in Ireland and Northern Ireland. One day we toured the Giant's Causeway and on another roadtrip, we headed west to the Galway areas of the island. This Airbnb became our first anchor that we built our remaining Irish itinerary around.

When we continued our trip into the UK, we had three places, or anchors, we absolutely wanted to visit; London, Liverpool and Glasgow over a six-week period. We landed a good housesit in Kent, which is about 90 minutes from London. When we got there, we realized it wouldn't be possible to go into London while taking care of the dog and the house. In addition, it was quite expensive for the two of us to travel round-trip by train into London. We'd wake up and walk Teddy, the Samoyed, then we'd head out to explore the local area. We enjoyed the Kent area, taking in Dover, Rochester, and Canterbury. While there, we continued to search for housesits elsewhere in the UK.

Meanwhile, we knew we really wanted to spend a week in Liverpool, and we wanted to stay in the city center. The chances of a housesit coming up with these wishes were slim, so we booked a month ahead for a week and got a weekly discount on our Liverpool stay. It was perfect, and our second anchor in the UK. Liverpool is a fantastic city full of incredible history, and of course, if you're a Beatles fan, it's a must-stop.

While enjoying Kent and Liverpool, a Glasgow housesit popped up, creating another anchor for us. We interviewed and secured a good housesit that was similar to our situation in Kent. But in this case, Glasgow, although 30 minutes away by train, was an affordable transit option. In addition, the owners were perfectly happy letting us leave their pup, Jessie the Sheltie, for up to 8 hours. Thus, we were able to enjoy Glasgow, Edinburgh, the Kelpies and even St Andrews.

For our last bit of UK geography, we wanted to explore Stonehenge and the Jurassic Trail. Crossing our fingers that a housesit would show up in the SW area of the UK that we could use as an anchor, we were very happy when, Bam! a super housesit in Bristol popped up. And guess what? The homeowner was the Director of Marketing at Stonehenge, and she gave us special passes to enjoy the site. We were also able to make day trips to the Jurassic Trail and hiked a good portion of it, one day at a time.

Thus, our overall UK + Ireland accommodation experience looked like this:
Total time in countries: 82 days
Total days in housesits: 41 days
Total days in Airbnb: 41 days

By splitting our time equally between the two options, we made the UK much more affordable. Our total accommodation expense for these 82 days was $4000.

Another Real Housesitting and Airbnb Strategy

We spent the winter in Mexico. Granted, Mexico's accommodation is much cheaper than that of the UK, but we also knew it was likely we could find a few charming housesits in the touristy areas of the country. On our list for Mexico were the following anchors:

- Puerto Vallarta
- Yucatan
- Lake Chapala area
- Butterfly migration
- Mexico City

Why did we have these particular anchors? We had many travel credits on Southwest Airlines, and Southwest flies to Puerto Vallarta from the US. We figured we would start there. There are several areas in the Yucatan we wanted to visit to test out as possible places to live long-term in the future. We had heard Lake Chapala was a great place for expats. I had always wanted to see the Monarch butterfly migration, and although I had spent a month in Mexico City, Steve hadn't and he wanted to visit the heartbeat of Mexico. So we threw our desires out to the serendipitous angels of travel to see which anchors would come back.

After waiting patiently and fretting a bit, our anchors dropped in. We found a super Airbnb in Puerto Vallarta away from the tourist district but in a great location for $40 a night with a monthly discount. In Akumal on the Yucatan, we landed a housesit with two dogs and a car, and then we also rented an

Airbnb for a month for $50 a night to extend our time in Cancun. We followed this with another incredible housesit in Ajijic on Lake Chapala. As for the butterfly migration, we went ahead and booked an Airbnb right on the edge of the butterfly preserve. And finally, since our kids wanted to visit us in Mexico City, we booked an Airbnb for $76 a night that would suit all of us so that we didn't have to worry about a housesit's house being big enough for the whole family.

Thus, our overall Mexico accommodation experience looked like this:
Total time in country: 119 days
Total days in housesits: 34 days
Total days in Airbnb: 85 days
By splitting our time one-third to two-thirds between the two options, we made Mexico stretch our budget even further. Our total accommodation spend for these 119 days was $3600 on an $8000 accommodation budget.

The Benefit of English-Speaking Countries for Nomads

As we worked our way through the first three months of our nomad life (first month, US; second month, Ireland; third month, UK), we realized we had accidentally done something miraculous, and we now recommend it as something you do intentionally. Even though we've traveled extensively throughout our lives together and as a couple, we haven't traveled as a nomad couple.

It's different.

There are new stressors and challenges we never imagined as nomads that we never encountered as tourists. Because we were in English-speaking countries, some of the stress of travel was less. We didn't have to struggle with language or too drastic changes in culture in order to get around logistically. This helped us settle into our nomad life quicker. We can't imagine how much more stressful our nomad life might have been at the beginning if we had started in a country where we didn't speak the language.

Some examples where knowing English and being able to read and speak English paid off included basic bus schedules, health information, train schedule changes, and Covid alerts. As vacationers, this information wasn't something we really paid attention to. But as full-time travelers, it controls our world. In non-English speaking countries, information that its citizens need is rarely in English. But tourism information, which is a different category altogether, often is.

Here's how being in an English-speaking country as nomads really helped us. In touristy areas, the transportation system is frequently written in English and the locals often speak English. But outside of those areas, getting around can be very complicated if you have to interpret signage and maps or ask for directions. Several times we got lost navigating local bus routes. Even though Google helped us get to and fro, being able to read local information sheets or talk to people got us out of many jams.

And speaking of jam, finding food in the grocery can be complicated. Groceries are arranged differently in different countries. They don't carry the same categories of foods, and labels are designed differently. We needed Band-aids. The local grocery didn't carry them, so we had to go to the drug store, which is different from a pharmacy. We also discovered that Band-aids are called plasters. We expected them to be with other first aid items, but we found them in toiletries. The reason we found them, though, was because everything was in English. It'd be so much more difficult in another language! And by the way, good luck finding real peanut butter!

The point is that the skills we needed to develop as nomads needed honing when we first set out. (They still do!) Learning to use new apps on our phones, finding wifi and asking for passwords, navigating streets versus avenues versus roads versus highways, and understanding groceries strengthened our travel chops. Starting in English made that easier.

Third Stop, Mexico

Once we decided to go to Mexico, and we got over the feeling of "going backward," we began looking at ways to get back across the Atlantic. Our new life of slow travel started to impact us with major "ah-ha" moments. If we can slow travel and take our time in countries, why can't we also take our time getting *to* countries as well? What's our hurry? Do we have to fly everywhere?

Repositioning Cruises

I stumbled upon the idea of repositioning cruises. Seasonally, the cruise industry must reposition its ships to take advantage of tourist trends. In the northern hemisphere's summer, they need their ships in the Mediterranean Sea and in Alaska. In the winter, they need to be in the Caribbean. So twice a year, ships take on one-way voyages to reposition themselves for the tourist seasons.

And guess what? With our daily budget at about $125, a repositioning cruise fits right into our monthly finances. We could either buy flights and fourteen nights of travel plus food and entertainment, or we could book a repositioning cruise from England to Mexico for about the same price as the flights plus hotels over fourteen days.

Thus, we booked our first repositioning cruise. It solved all of our needs. It'd get us out of the cold weather, get us across the Atlantic, get us to warm weather, and the costs were in budget. Plus, we wouldn't have jet lag when we got to Mexico. It was a win-win-win.

By the way, I talked with several experts in the cruising industry and learned there really are no differences among websites in regards to your final cruise price. Although each website offers different types of incentives including on-board credits, free flights, and free excursions, the value of these offers across the websites is equally the same. The cruise lines intentionally do this so that there are competitive advantages among the cruise lines in incentives, but ultimately no one has a cheaper price overall. So find the website, including the cruise websites, that offers the incentives you want (we like on-board credit), and book. We usually use AAA.com.

The Nomad Day-to-Day Living Stage

As we go through our day-day-to-day life, we have developed a pattern for enjoying each week. In a typical week, we go out 3-4 days of the week to enjoy the local activities. A few days a week we try to get together with friends, and on Tuesdays, we work on logistics, manage money, negotiate our life, and thrive. Some of the new things we need to concentrate on that are unique to our nomad life revolve around the "how" of our life.

Picking our Next Destination

When we get ready to go to new countries, we first go to the US Dept of State website, then we go to the country's website, then we check in to various Facebook groups. At the Facebook groups, we'll triangulate and verify information regarding what local border agents expect and then make our final decisions about whether we'll travel.

Securing Visas

While we think and dream about our next trips, we're also always thinking about the visas we might need. Visas take a lot of work and planning. Depending on the country and your citizenship, the rules vary. Some countries allow you to get the visa when you land, but for other countries, it's quite complex.

When we took our around-the-world trip where we visited 6 countries in 30 days, we found out we would need both Chinese and Russian visas. It was a complicated mess. Each country required a slew of paperwork which included letters of invitation, passport photos, hotel reservations, flight reservations and itineraries. Some of these things we knew; others we were doing on the fly.

In order to get the Chinese and Russian visas, we had to submit our passports to their embassies in the US. One embassy was in Houston, the other in San Francisco. We had to use the embassy that's attached to our address. China put Colorado in the west, while Russia put Colorado in the Central US...resulting in two different embassy cities for us to use. Each Visa would take about a month to get, so we had to time them to our departures. In addition, during the Visa process, the embassies could require us to visit at a moment's notice.

Rather than risking a mess up between the embassies and costly, potential trips to them for Steve, our daughter, and me, we hired a visa company to manage the paperwork. Through AAA, we got discounts for the procedures. Travisa, the company we hired, would be able to get both sets of visas done and would represent us, if necessary, at the appropriate embassy. For only $20-30 processing fee for each passport, it was well worth the fee and relieved a lot of the headache for us. But despite planning ahead and doing everything correctly, our combined visa totals for the three of us were almost $1000. Be sure to plan your visa expenses into your budget or possibly visit somewhere else and avoid expensive visas all together.

Visas in the European Union

As US citizens travel in Europe, things are about to change. Currently, we don't need a Visa to visit the EU, but that's changing in 2023, and we'll have to apply for a Visa online to visit a select list of countries that are known as

"Schengen Zone" countries. What's the Schengen Zone? It's a collective set of countries, mostly in the European Union. US Citizens can only stay in Schengen Zone countries for 90 days over a 180 day rolling period. In 2022, the 90-day rule will still apply, but we'll also need to register at ETIAS.

A Real-Live Example of Our Schengen Time

Remember at the beginning of our story how we were going to go to Costa Rica first and end up in Ireland last? And how did that plan change? Change is the name of the game when you're full-time travelers. This is how we have managed our first year on the road.

August 15. Arrived in Ireland. It has a special category in the EU and it's not in Schengen, so we didn't have to count days. US citizens can stay in Ireland for 90 days.

Sept 6. Arrived in the UK. Also not in the EU and not in Schengen, US citizens can stay for 6 months.

Nov 3. Left on a cruise out of Southampton.

Nov 4. Spent one day in France.

Nov 5. Spent one day in Spain.

Nov 6. Spent one day in Portugal.

Nov 11. Spent one day in Bermuda. Bermuda is not in the EU nor in Schengen, US citizens can stay 30 days.

Nov 16. Spent two days in USA

Nov 18. Arrived in Mexico. Spent 120 days. US Citizens can spend 180 days.

Mar 6. Spent two days in USA

Mar 18. Arrived in the UK. Spent one day.

Mar 19. Arrived in Spain.

April 1. Arrived in Italy.

May 1. Arrived in Portugal.

June 18. Flew to a non-Schengen country, Croatia. At this point, we needed to stay out of the Schengen Zone for 90 days. So we toured Croatia, Montenegro and Albany.

Sept 19. Returned to France, Austria, and Malta for the next 180 rolling days of our Schengen time.

Nov 16. Arrived in Venice to catch a repositioning cruise to South Africa

Dec 15. Arrived in South Africa for the rest of the year.

Passports

We are both terrified of losing our passports. Steve and I both keep them in ziploc, waterproof baggies to protect them from the elements. Inside of it are our COVID vaccination cards and our yellow WHO vaccination cards. We have copies of them in our backpacks, and we keep additional copies of them in the cloud.

Important Paperwork to Carry with You

Deciding what paperwork you'll need to bring with you as you travel is difficult. We put all of our important papers into a safe deposit box. Prior to locking it all away, we took photos of each item and stored the photos in Google Drive so we'd always have access. These important papers included our marriage license, legal documents regarding my name, and my child's birth certificate.

In the time of COVID, our COVID vaccine cards are worth the price of gold. We've taken pictures of them in case we lose them. But we've yet to find anyone globally that accepts the pictures as evidence of vaccination. Thus, we carry the cards with us inside our passports. Both the cards and the passports stay in zip-tight, waterproof envelopes.

As for prescriptions, we do the same: we have paper copies of them from our doctors and then we take photocopies and store them up in Google. Sometimes, global pharmacies will use the label from our bottles. Other times, we've shown our paper copies, and they've been accepted. But often, we need to see local doctors to get local scripts of our meds.

Money, Cash and Credit Cards

I am a bit fanatical about managing our credit and debit cards when we travel. I've had cards go lost and go fraudulent, leaving me without any access to money until I could get new ones. Fortunately, I had friends with me who lent me money until I could get myself sorted. Being in a foreign country without access to my own money was very scary. So I built up a financial security blanket so that if I ever end up in that situation again, I can recover quickly.

Our Debit/Credit Card Set Up

As we have traveled the world, both of us have had credit cards go fraudulent. When this happens, the credit card agencies cancel cards and reissue new cards with new numbers. The problem is that they will only send the cards to our address on file. If we try to change our address on file, it backfires. Since our address on file is in the US, we have to wait until the card arrives at our mail service then have the mail service scan it so that we have the numbers, then have the mail service forward it via FedEx or similar to our international location. At best, this can be done in a week. Most likely it will take 3-4 weeks.

Therefore, when our credit cards go fraud, we activate our back up cards. One great benefit of using Google Pay with Chase is that the new credit card will automatically load in our phones almost immediately. Thus, we can continue to use our phones for credit card transactions as long as on one asks to see the actual card.

As for our debit cards, when these go fraud or are lost, it's more difficult to replace them. Like credit cards, the issuing bank automatically cancels the debit card and reissues it. They also reissue a PIN which comes separately in the mail. Getting these two documents, like above in the credit card scenario, is twice as complicated. Schwab is very good about getting debit cards replaced quickly, and they will overnight new cards to you regardless of where you are. This is a huge benefit and one we've used successfully.

What's in Our Wallets

Steve and I each carry our own sets of credit cards, debit cards and IDs. If we get separated, kidnapped, or lost, we have our own tools to get ourselves back together again. We do not have combined credit card accounts for these reasons. In addition, we carry our "wallets" in three different places in case of theft.

Wallet One in purse
Passport
Schwab Debit Card
Chase Sapphire Card (also on phone)

Wallet Two in backpack
Copy of Passport

EdwardJones Debit Card

Chase Bonvoy Card (also on phone)

Wallet Three in luggage

Drivers License

Axos Bank Debit Card

American Express Blue Travel Card (also on phone)

Bank of America Travel Rewards Card

We use these particular debit cards (Schwab, Axos, EdJones) because they do not charge for ATM withdrawals anywhere. The credit cards have no transaction fees and give tons of mileage/point rewards. Please use our referral links to get your credit cards. Both you and we will get bonus points.

When/How to Get Cash

Depending on the country we're in, the amount of cash we need varies. In Europe, we hardly use cash, but in Mexico, we use a ton. Regardless, we use the same strategy for our first cash withdrawal with our debit card. We do something that most people advise against because many folks think the fees charged at airports are high. They aren't. The minute we land in the airport, we go to the ATM in the airport and withdraw enough cash for a week. We then buy a bottle of water so that we have small bills that we'll need almost the minute we leave the airport for busses, taxes, tips, etc. Once you leave the airport, ATMs can be hard to find or they are often out of money, and you can be left stranded or having to pay a higher rate to an exchange house. Use the ATM in the airport and call it a day.

If we need more money while we're in the country, we'll get it from a bank's ATM. By the time a week has passed, we have a better understanding of our cash vs credit card purchases, and we've most likely located a safe ATM that is reliable and contains cash.

Finally, whenever the credit card machine or the ATM asks if you want the currency rate computed locally or in your home currency, always say locally. It's cheaper.

Credit Card Hacking

You may have heard that there are many ways to use credit cards to get "free" travel such as free flights, hotel rooms, and cruises. This is true. The main way to get these free perks is by signing up for credit cards and getting bonus points for signing up. We regularly rotate through 6-10 credit cards in order to bank lots of credit card points to help underwrite our travel expenses. Rather than recreate all of that information here, we'd rather point you to folks who travel hack full-time and have incredible strategies and advice. Start with the following resources:

Frequent Miler
Doctor of Credit
Nomadic Matt

Cash Flow and Paying Bills

Between the two of us, we have at least six different credit cards. Prior to our nomad life, we had our own bank accounts too, and we kept our finances separate due to the separate ways we arrived at our collective retirement portfolio. Although we still keep our own cards and our own bank accounts, we made a few changes.

On the 29th of the month, we have our personal banks transfer money into a Schwab checking account that is in both of our names. We deposit the same amount of money. We have asked our credit card companies to make sure our due dates are all on the 15th of the month so that everything is due all at once, making tracking easier and we have auto pay set up for our credit cards.

On the 4th of the month, we sit down and review our various credit card bills. If necessary, we pay any bills not paid through autopay via Schwab Bill Pay. Therefore, we don't have to print statements and mail checks. Finally, Steve combines all of our credit card statements into one spreadsheet. He streamlines the categorizations of the items to see how much we're spending in each category. We look at outliers and inliers and determine if we're spending money in the way that we budget, making slight adjustments as we go. So far, we've stayed within our annual budget, although some months are higher or lower than the monthly budget.

Cell Phones, Computers and Other Gadgets for Nomad Life

Our new life needed new tools. After many trips and locations, we have figured out the best tools for us.

When we first started traveling, we made many errors with tools. For cell phones, we purchased our providers' international plans and came away with bad service and high bills. For computers, we lugged too large laptops because we were still in "work mode" and wanted big screens. And for all the other gadgets, we brought the wrong gear many times.

Cell Phone Service

Whereas you'll see many people write about getting a Sim card when they arrive in the country, we have resisted doing this. After trying every international cell plan under the sun over time, we settled on Google Fi, Google's cell phone service. Sadly, Google Fi is only available for US residents. The one thing that makes Google Fi brilliant is that it works the second we land on the tarmac without any hassle. And what do we need the second we land on the tarmac? An internet connection so we can figure out where and how to get somewhere. *This flexibility is priceless.*

I have been using Google Fi for three years. In that time, I have traveled to 37 countries and all 50 US states. The only time I have ever had any trouble with Google Fi is in my basement in Denver, in the backcountry of West Virginia, the middle of the Pacific Ocean, on the reservations through Arizona, and in the Amazon in Peru.

After three years, I absolutely recommend Google Fi with a Pixel. You can get a $25 credit on Google Fi with my referral.

Google Fi Versus Verizon

With all my social media posts, photo uploads, video uploads via Instagram and Boomerang, I have never had a problem in any country, including China, with Google Fi. On the other hand, before Steve switched, he used a Samsung S9 with Verizon's TravelPass and had horrible experiences. He couldn't access apps, WIFI was inconsistent, and often could not get on the internet. He couldn't get his texts either. *Every time he suffered on Verizon, I had access on Google Fi.* In a Verizon vs Google Fi contest, Fi won every time.

Google Fi After Six Months Abroad

We had heard rumors that Google Fi will drop your data plan if you've been out of the USA for longer than six months. It's true. We got a warning letter that they would stop our data until we returned to the USA. Well, we weren't returning, so we had to come up with a different solution. While we still ascertain that Google Fi is a good choice, if you won't be returning to the USA frequently, it's a plan to avoid.

Nonetheless, our friends at Geeksteamers, shared their way to get around the Google Fi's six-month limit by using e-Sims. We ended up moving our Google Fi number to Google Voice for our phone calls and text messages. We purchased a global data plan through Flexiroam, and all is working well.

Phones

Steve has a Samsung and I have a Pixel. Their cameras are so good that we do not carry extra cameras with us.

Computers

We each carry a laptop with us. Although we know couples who only carry one, we can't imagine it. We love being able to explore our own topics in our own time, and we feel that the weight and risks of carrying two computers are worth it. I love my Dell Inspirion 13 5000.

WiFi Router

We use a WiFi Router (this one) when we're in coffee shops or in the general public. It's especially important when we do our banking. In addition, we add a VPN to improve security while on open networks. On cruises, where we must pay for internet service by device, we use our router. It counts as one device even though we connect both our phones, our computers and our Kindles to it. By the way, make sure you have a router and a VPN service when you're doing any banking internationally. We've had several scenarios, especially in the Americas, where banking websites simply wouldn't work until we used a US-based ISP created through a VPN. Use our referral link to get the Cyberghost VPN. If the link is expired, let me know, and I'll send you a new one.

EReaders

We both love our Kindles. We download free ebooks from Freebooksy.com and also use our local library at home to borrow books.

Cameras

We don't carry extra cameras beyond our phones. Whereas in the past we lugged an SLR or two, we finally admitted that our cell phones are good enough. All we do with the photos is post them to social media, and Facebook doesn't need professional quality photos.

WhatsApp

WhatsApp is a messenger service where you can make phone calls and send texts. It's free. It's the workshorse of our communication strategy with not only our family and friends in the US, but basically everyone else outside of the US. We've yet to find a business, service, or person outside of the US that doesn't use WhatsApp. Install it before you leave the US. One caveat is that the person you're calling must also use WhatsApp. We had a heck of a time convincing some family and friends to install it.

Google Translate

When we travel in places where we don't know the language, we use three strategies. The first is to learn some of the local terms to help us get by. We always research the following words and phrases, and we memorize them then use them as often as we can.

- Hello
- Goodbye
- Thank you
- Good morning
- Excuse me
- I'm sorry
- I'm from the US
- Can you help me
- Do you speak English
- The numbers 1-10, 100, 1000
- You are so kind
- Do you speak Spanish? (My second language)

If we need more communication, we use our second strategy: we will ask if someone speaks English. As our third strategy, we use Google Translate on our phones.

The Love Story Continues

As we come to almost a year on the road and this book goes to publish, we thought we'd add a few thoughts on things we've learned while being nomads.

Stuff: No matter how much you bring, and for us we only have two carry-on suitcases and two backpacks, you're still bringing too much. It seems after each month, we are still reorganizing and rearranging our things. We dump about 10 percent of our stuff each time we rearrange.

More Stuff: We still have the desire to buy things because they're pretty or we like them. But we follow a one-in, one-out rule. If we buy something, it replaces something else. Otherwise, we won't have room for it. In addition, charity shops around the world often have exactly what we need. Finding an item is half the fun and provides activities for the day. Steve got a brand new pair of Patagonia shorts in a Mexican charity shop for $4.

Planning: Refuse the urge to plan too much. We find that we have to restrain ourselves from planning too far in advance. After all, planning is part of the fun. Now we chunk our planning time into 90-day blocks around geography. Within that 90 days, we try to housesit for half of it and stay in Airbnbs for the other half of the time.

Balancing Accommodations: Balancing decision making around Airbnb versus housesits is still tough. The challenge is that good housesits may appear just a week before they're available whereas a good Airbnb gets booked more than 90 days in advance. The magic is knowing when to book an Airbnb so we get a good one versus missing out on a great housesit that shows up at the last minute. If we don't particularly care exactly where we'll be staying, we wait longer to make decisions, thus giving time for good housesits to appear.

Toothpaste: 100 ml toothpaste sneaks through airport security checks.

Hacking Kitchens: Before going grocery shopping, assess what's in the kitchen already and build your meal prep around some of those ingredients. It'll save you time and money.

Strangers to Friends: When someone says "if you're in our town…", take down their names and numbers and take them up on their offers. We've met some amazing people and had wonderful experiences.

Leashes: During the initial call with a housesitter, ask if the dogs are good on leashes.

Health Care: Health care is affordable almost everywhere except the US. And it's good, too.

Why: As we travel the world, the question of "why" resonates with us every day. Yes, we want to explore other cultures, try new foods, see great art, hike wonderful mountains, meet amazing people and improve the world, but why? Why are we doing this and what is its purpose? How can we consume the world but not do it consumptively? Our "why" is becoming much more important and identified.

Peace: We are doing this to bring peace to the world. When we get to know one another, we want to help and be friends, not divide and conquer.

Prejudice: For us, every new encounter requires us to go inward and reevaluate our prejudices, our likes and our dislikes. Before going into the International Slave Museum in Liverpool, I thought Black Lives Matter and the history of institutional racism was just an American thing. Not true. The whole world is struggling with issues of colonialism, identity, and history. I've rethought how the stream of education that came through my brain was created by a colonial might effusing colonial ideas through the English language and western economics. I even worked for the company that propagated this content and had a mission to cover the world in English. Now, I wonder, what is my responsibility to the world to open up paths for other points of view about the world's history and its future?

The News: Subscribe to one national newspaper to keep on top of national issues, especially COVID. We get the digital version of the *New York Times* and ignore almost all other US news venues.

Existing Relationships and Friendships: When we moved to Denver, one of my goals was to establish a good set of friends. Through the hiking and walking communities, I found an awesome set of girlfriends whom I regularly hiked and played with. I cherished these friendships and nurtured them over the eight years we lived in Denver. Steve developed a group of poker buddies who played their hands weekly, and together, we found our niche of friendships to improve our lives.

As we've traveled, these friendships have changed. Time zones inhibit virtual poker games and girlfriend chats. I'll occasionally drop postcards to the girls, and I'm sure to comment on social media when they post pictures of themselves with each other. But the day-to-day interactions are now gone; we have to schedule zoom calls and chats in order to stay connected.

Communication: The communication between Steve and me has changed immensely. Now more than ever, we have to communicate about a lot of things. Everything we do requires planning and logistics just to get out the door. Throw in eating, touring, and recreating, and it's double the effort. Add in another language and Google Translate, and there's an extra level of dimension to communication that we've never had before.

Our Relationship: As we explore each country and each other, we find we're getting closer and really understanding the power of our partnership. Never before have we felt so close to another person. We know where our skills complement each other (logistics and travel) and where one set is stronger than another's (language and directions.) We're learning our weaknesses, too, like cooking good meals and exercising patience.

Romance: It helps that we like each other and we're best friends, too. Just like at home, though, on the road we have to make time for romance. Even though our daily life includes lots of eating out and exploring new locations, we still have to find "date time." We actually state when we're on dates and plan them outside of our regular planning and logistics. Sometimes our day-to-day relationship needs the spark of date night.

New Friends: We're also realizing that in our new life, we have new goals and new priorities. Finding friends remains high on our list, but now we have to find friends in different ways and in different locations. Thank goodness for Facebook! We use it to find activities and events in the local area, connect with other like-minded nomads, and find locals and expats in our new locations willing to meet us and make friends. In addition, when we cruise, we make sure to eat dinner at shared tables so we can meet others. Although we don't think of ourselves as cruisers, we have lots in common with those who do.

As we make our way through the world, we want to expand our friendships and how we understand the world. Here is what we do in each location we live in, keeping in mind our personal goals of fitness, language, healthy eating and volunteering.

Nomad Friends: Our new life is weird. As we got ready to leave and explained to our friends about our plans, many of them just couldn't understand. They'd gasp or roll their eyes and state things like, "We could *never* do that!" So now, it's really no surprise that our conversations have become kind of irrelevant to them. Although they enjoy hearing our exploits because we're friends and the exploits are interesting, we just don't relate as much as we used to. We have found it's important to find like-minded people doing the things we're doing. It's nice to have conversations with people where we don't have to explain our life over and over again. Thus, we turn to many virtual scenarios to create these friends.

Nomad friends aren't necessarily Americans, and they aren't necessarily expats. We have nomad friends who are on a 5-year road trip through the US. We have others who only nomad a portion of the year. We even have "nomad" friends who aren't yet traveling, but are thinking about it and are in the nomad mindset. Nonetheless, we find that when we talk to these friends, we share travel stories, tips and tricks, relationship hacks, and adventure dreams together.

Alone Time: Sometimes we need our own alone time. We've gotten into the habit of giving each other space in the morning as both of us like to meditate and write when we wake up. Sometimes, we work out together, too. We do try to eat a late breakfast together so we can settle into our day's plans.

Staying Active: Beside the things we need to do to live, we have a whole world of things to do while we're in a location. Before arriving at a location, we research what we'll do and how we'll do it. We love to find fitness and dance classes, free things to do at the library, hiking groups, vegan get-togethers, and walking tours. Facebook, Meetup, and Eventbrite are our go-to places to find things to do.

Our Love Story

This love story started when I was a kid, suffering through family road trips in the back seat with a sister who never liked me. At one time, I documented our family's troubles and joys through travel writing, punctuating the narrative with torn ticket stubs and highlighted TripTiks. The love of travel writing developed because I fell in love with traveling, despite the crazy antics of my dad's perspective. I wanted to share the world through words. When I met a man who also loved traveling, and we found out we were travel compatible, a world opened up. I could travel, write about it, and enjoy it with a man who loved me and traveling as well. This love story, the most perfect love story ever told, continues. I hope you'll follow along and enjoy the ride as we continue this journey.

This past weekend, Steve and I enjoyed one of Latin America's greatest weekly events, the Ciclovia. In the major cities, the recreation departments close the main thoroughfares, opening the streets up to outdoor recreation. People grab their bikes, skateboards, rollerblades, and family members and get outside for some exercise. On a perfectly sunny and beautiful day, we rented bikes, circling Mexico's Chapultepec Park and riding the Paseo de la Reforma. We stopped at the Angel de Glorieta, sitting on her steps for a short break. Steve looked at me and said, "My love, we have an incredible life. I am so happy you said yes to me eleven years ago. Thank you." I dabbed my eyes, gave him a smooch, and responded, "I love you, too."

Follow Us on Social Media

If it weren't for social media, we could not have this lifestyle. We find so many helpful people, tips and tricks through Twitter, Facebook, Pinterest, and Instagram. We share and follow back, so please find us and engage with us. If we're in your town, please reach out. We'd love to grab a cuppa with you. We also hope you'll subscribe to our YouTube channel and our newsletter. Thanks so much. @EatWalkLearn

Facebook

Pinterest

Instagram

Twitter

Website

YouTube

Newsletter

Two Carry-Ons and a Plan: The Workbook

You're read our love story and seen a real-live example of how we went from thinking about our retirement with no idea what we'd do to formulating it, writing it down, and actually executing our nomad strategy. We documented the process and the questions we asked ourselves as we went from the Planning Stage to the Day-to-Day Stage. You'll find all the to-do lists, checklists, and timelines you might need to get your plan off and out the door. We wish you only the best of fun as you figure it all out. You start with the Planning Stage.

As you work through this part of the book, you'll find the headings roughly follow those in the Love Story portion of the book. If you need real-world examples of what we were thinking and how we were processing each stage and step, flip back over to the front of the book for inspiration.

The Planning Stage

Before actually setting a date to start your travel life, there's pre-work to do.

Step 1: Have a Vision

As you get ready to travel full time, you'll need to think about a variety of things. Your answers to these questions will set the tone for how you'll do the logistics of your life. Once you answer the first set of questions, it will trigger an entire new set. Don't worry, take each question, one at a time, and work your way through them. There are no wrong answers, and it's likely you'll change your mind many times. Start with these questions:

1. What do you want to see when you travel? Sculpture, the Seven Wonders, canyons, snow, beaches, orchestras, books?

2. Is there a temperature range you'll want to stay in? Are you searching for an endless summer?

3. Will you carry a backpack or check your luggage? Is it important to you that you have the right outfit everytime or can you make a few wardrobe pieces work for all occasions?

4. Are there particular countries you want to see? Or avoid?

5. Will you have a "project" to do like genealogy, follow world battles, or find the best wool skeins?

6. Are you okay with not knowing the language, or do you want to only stay in countries that speak your language?

Step 2: Convince Your Spouse and Family

If you're going to travel with someone, you may have some convincing to do. Or you may have to give your partner some time to digest your idea. You may need to modify and adapt.

Then, you'll need to tell your family. Telling your family that you're retiring is one thing. Telling them that you're selling the house and everything in it, permanently packing, and traveling the world is another. They'll be worried about three things:

1. Your safety.
2. Your connection and obligations to the family.
3. Your money.

Be sure to have your answers ready and firm. Sometimes a well-meaning family can knock a plan too far into the future, if at all. Be ready for them to project their fears on you. Even if they are totally supportive, their ability to instill fear and guilt could derail the best laid plans. Be firm. Be kind. Be compassionate. Then continue planning.

Hopefully, your conversation will flow as easily as ours did. But you may have worrying parents, older aunts and uncles, or cousins with whom you're really close. If so, make sure you establish the communication you will have with them, and you might even discuss how you'll do major holidays and events. Let them know that you're really only a phone call away. At any point, you could return if necessary, or they can come visit you in one of your new destinations. Go through the what Ifs and mock up plans with the answers. You'll need to ease their anxiety about your travels. The best way to ease anxiety is with communication and information.

Step 3: A Rough Idea of a Plan

Now that you have a vision and you've talked with your family, you need a rough plan. At this point, you'll draw a line in the sand. It starts with a date that you leave your home and head out into the world. You'll answer the mobility, geography and theme questions, too. For example, you may decide that you'll travel by train through the US to see all the baseball stadiums. Or you'll camp in the national parks of the world. Or you'll fly to the airports that have the initials of all your family members. Whatever it is, mark a date on the calendar. This is the date you'll start planning backwards from. Because once you can see yourself leaving your home, everything starts to fall into place.

Step 4: Get Your Affairs in Order

If you don't already have your will, power of attorney and other life-ending documents in order, now is the time. It can be grim. But the truth is, when you've gotten rid of all of your stuff and you've written your will, you'll feel light-hearted and ready to go. So contact an attorney, work through the particulars, organize your banking, and designate your beneficiaries and executors. These things can take time due to some decisions you'll need to make, people you'll need to communicate with, and any change of states you might be making. Start now.

The Disposal Stage

The first step of the disposal stage is to stop buying stuff. Don't buy anything else unless you can eat it or bring it with you. You may start this stage up to two years before you leave. If people insist on giving you gifts, ask for gift cards to things like Amazon, Viator, an airline or a hotel chain. Anything you buy after you've decided to leave just becomes something else you'll need to make a plan to get rid of....so, stop buying things!

Now that you've stopped buying things, you can formally start The Disposal Stage. This stage is all about the decisions you'll make to get rid of your stuff. You'll need to start with the end in mind to get rid of your stuff. If you decide what you'll keep and what you'll get rid of, you'll be able to work through the next set of steps easier. First you'll need to decide how you will carry the stuff you want to bring with you.

How Will You Carry Your Stuff?

Break down your action plan of what to bring by starting with the end in mind.

1. How will you carry your stuff?
2. What type of luggage do you want? Hard side? Soft side? Duffle? Wheeled? Checked or Carry-on? Backpack? Day pack?

3. What stuff will you bring? Tents? Clothes? Shoes? Sleeping pads? Yoga mats? Hats? Rain coats? Jackets? Shorts? Sweaters? Pants? Dressy things? Casual things? Socks? Sandals?

4. Will you keep any stuff in a storage unit?

5. Will you keep or sell your house?

Luggage and Backpacks

It's a personal choice on how you'll carry your stuff. Some people like duffels, some like checked bags, some like large backpacks.

Checked Bags or Carry-on Bags?

Here are some things to consider when deciding on your luggage setup:

1. Will you check your baggage or carry it on?

2. If you'll be flying often, are you prepared to roll your bag many thousands of steps to get it on the plane?

3. Can you lift your bag?

4. Even if you check your bag, you'll have hundreds of staircases and steps to get from the terminal to your hotel. Many places don't have elevators. Can you manage it yourself? Are you willing to pay for porters?

5. Do you want to pay for checked bags over and over again?

6. Do you have large or oversized items?

7. If your luggage got lost, what would you do?

8. Do you have cameras and other gear that you can't or won't check?

9. What else do you need to personally carry?

Wheeled Backpacks or Non-Wheeled Backpacks

When looking at backpacks, think of these questions:

1. Do you carry a water bottle?
2. Do you need lumbar support?
3. Do you need a waist belt?
4. Do you need reflective material?
5. Do you have keys or fobs you need to have quick access to?
6. Will you carry a computer that needs a padded sleeve?
7. Should you get a rain cover?
8. Will your backpack carry all of your stuff or should you go smaller and get a day pack?
9. Can your back handle up to 50 pounds for an entire day for multiple days?
10. Can you lift 50 pounds over your head?
11. Do you want wheels for when you don't want to carry it?

Should You Sell or Rent Out Your Home?

Getting rid of your stuff includes your house! Work through the following questions about the decision to rent out your home or to sell it *without* focusing on the financial side of the picture:

1. Do you like the house?
2. Do you still need this house?
3. Do you want to return to where you live?
4. Do you want to be homeowners?
5. Is it a good time to sell?
6. If you do buy another home elsewhere, what are the criteria for that house purchase?

Now add the financial picture into the questioning strategy.

1. Do you need rental income in your portfolio?
2. Do you want to manage a house (even with a management company) from afar?
3. Do you want a reason to return to your city?
4. Are you prepared for the unexpected expenses of homeownership?
5. What will you do with the proceeds of the house sale?
6. Are there tax consequences you're willing to bear?

Often the answers won't be clear cut. You might change your mind several times. But nailing this decision down will guide everything else you have to decide about your stuff. If you keep the house, there's a place to keep your stuff, too. You can rent your place furnished and you'll only need to find a place for your personal items. If you sell, you'll need to get rid of all your personal items or get a storage unit.

Should You Get a Storage Unit?

Making the decision to get a storage unit is complicated. By getting a storage unit, you don't have to process the feelings that come up when you get rid of stuff like your heirlooms and family pictures. But if you decide not to have one, you'll have to take additional time to not only find homes for your stuff, but you'll have to feel the flood of emotions that come your way. Here are some questions to think about when making the storage unit decision.

1. What would you put in it?
2. Where will it be?
3. How much will it cost? Quarterly? Annually? Total over time?

4. If you pay for storage for a year, is the stuff in it worth that amount financially?

5. Could you replace the contents for less than the price of storage?

6. If you have heirlooms, do the kids really want them? Have you asked? If they want them later, why not take them now? If they won't want them, what's the real reason you're keeping them?

7. If your house burnt down, what would you really miss that isn't replaceable?

8. Would you rather have new stuff in your new life?

9. If you'll eventually settle somewhere, are you willing to pay to have the contents shipped to your new location?

10. Do you want to worry about the storage unit?

11. How will you insure the contents? Are you willing to pay this expense too?

Review the items in your house, determine what you can live without for a year, and make a plan to get rid of the "good stuff." The good stuff, such as heirlooms and artwork, can be hard to sell, and it might be better to give it away.

By now in the process, you should have answered the big questions, and you can create your action plan. The big three questions are:

1. How will you carry your stuff?

2. Will you keep your home?

3. Will you have a storage unit?

When you have these answers, you can focus on the next step. It's all about the "Good Stuff."

One Year Before Departure: What's the Good Stuff?

The "Good Stuff" in your home is the set of items that will be the hardest to let go of and also might be some of the hardest pieces to sell. They're unique items that require specialized buyers if you want to get the most amount of money for these items. How do you decide what the good stuff is? Ask these questions:

1. Is it good because it's expensive or there's emotional attachment to it?
2. If it burned in a fire, what would you do?
3. Are you looking for a good home for it or a good price?
4. Do you need appraisals to sell it?
5. Do you have buyers for it?
6. Do family members want it? Are you sure?
7. Has a family member asked for it?
8. Should it be donated to a museum?
9. What will make you happiest to get rid of it?
10. Are you willing to deal with picky buyers in order to get a good price for it?
11. Do you have the time and skills to sell it?

Six Months Before Departure: Make a Plan for the "Estate Sale/Garage Sale" Stuff

At six months out, make a plan to get rid of everything you don't need in the next six months. Your goal here is to get rid of waste, broken items, trash, and excess. What's left is the "Estate Sale/Garage Sale Stuff." When going through the remaining stuff in the house, ask yourself these questions:

1. Do you need twenty cups or just three?
2. Do you need your winter clothes or can you get rid of them now?
3. Are you still using it?
4. Are you waiting for a season or a holiday to pass before disposing of it?
5. Do you need all of it? All your baking bowls or just one? All five spatulas or can you get by with one?
6. Do you play all your CDs or just one or two?

Make piles or set aside a room to put these items. Take an honest look at the collective bunch and evaluate your energy levels. How much effort and time do you want to put into getting rid of the next group of stuff? Ask yourself these questions about the "garage sale stuff":

1. Are you willing to interact with lots of buyers?
2. Do you want to list your items for sale in multiple locations?
3. Are you willing to have a garage sale? Does your HOA even allow it?
4. Do you want to get rid of stuff or make the most amount of money for it? These are conflicting needs and require different amounts of time and effort.
5. Do you want someone else to manage the disposal of these items?

Many places will take your donations, but make sure you're donating things of value and not broken items you don't want to take the time or money to fix. Here are just a few places to consider when donating your items:

- Women's Shelters
- No Kill Pet Shelters
- Veterans Shelters
- Nursing Homes

- Adult Ed Programs
- Public Radio
- Recycle Centers
- Big Brother/Big Sisters
- Scouts
- Senior Centers

Garage Sales, Craigslist, Marketplace, or Estate Sellers?

You'll have to decide how much effort you want to spend to dispose of your things and how much time you have. If you have the time to take on the tedious task of garage sales and classified ads, great. If not, you might want to consider an Estate Seller.

Estate Sellers come to your house, evaluate the entire lot of goods, negotiate a percentage they'll take in cash from the total sale of all goods, categorize and organize your goods, sell the items, and collect and pay the sales tax. They do all the marketing, staging, and people managing. You don't even have to be in the house on the day(s) of the sale. For us, this was worth giving up 40-50% of the sale, especially since the Estate Sellers know the value of a half a bottle of Windex and a limited edition print from a local artist.

Arrange for Trash Items

While you're thinking and organizing how you'll get rid of all your stuff, you'll ultimately have trash and unwanted items in your house. You'll have to get rid of these things, too. If your city has an "extra garbage day" pick up service, find out when it is. Schedule your estate sale the week before the extra garbage day and/or prior to your escrow closing day. Timing is critical here.

Three-Six Months Before Departure: The Stuff Attached to Emotions

While you wait for your garage sales or estate sale, there are a few items you might want to spend extra time concentrating on. Most things in this category are attached to emotions. We found out in this phase that emotions really crept in and doubt surfaced. It was hard to dispose of things we'd had most of our lives. Our emotions cracked. But we focused on the end and powered through each decision. Allow yourself plenty of time for grieving in this phase.

Yearbooks

Call the school where the yearbooks come from and see if they want them. If not, the local libraries or historical societies might. If you're active on Facebook, post that you want to donate your yearbooks. Often classmates who have lost theirs may want yours.

Photos, Photo Albums, and Video

Digitize all your photos, videos, and photo albums. You can do one page at a time rather than each picture. Put them in the cloud like on Google Photos. Trash the albums. Digitizing everything takes lots of time. Not only does the physical work take time, but you need to allow for your emotional time too. Vacation snapshots are easier to throw out than wedding photos and grandparent events. If you think your kids want them, ask. Ours wanted a few but not the entire lot. Digital access was all they requested. If you don't have the time or skill, hire someone to do it for you. Get started soon, as it takes more time than you think.

China and Glassware

It's hard to fathom, but no one wants your china. You will not get any real money for it either. My 12-place setting Noritake China went in the Estate Sale, and I fetched a whopping $20 for the entire set. If you'd rather donate your China set than see it go for pennies, give it to a women's shelter to use as daily service ware.

Plants

Give your plants away to the local gardening clubs or contact them and have them come pick them up. Also see if they want any fertilizers, pesticides or potting soil you may also have in the garage or gardening shed.

Clothing

After you pack your suitcases with the clothing you want to take, the rest can go in the garage/estate sale. Clothing draws people to sales. Although you won't fetch the retail value on your clothing, people like to buy used clothes. Consider your clothing as a "loss leader" to get people to come to your sales. If you don't want to hassle selling one piece at a time, there are many places you can donate clothing such as:

- Women's Shelters
- Dress for Success Programs
- High School Prom Closets
- Senior Homes
- Charity Shops
- Nurseries
- No-Kill Animal Shelters
- Fundraisers and Church Bazaars

Pets

Please note that we are not advocating the irresponsible disposal of pets. If you do have to rehome your pet, look to rehoming agencies such as those organized around particular breeds or locations. Perhaps family or friends can take your pet. Please look for no-kill shelters and possibly even provide a fund to take care of your pet until it finds a home.

It's very hard to give up a pet. If your pet is large, it's likely you won't be able to bring her. Otherwise, if you are lucky enough to bring your pet along, get your pet passports, carriers, vaccines, and food organized now for a less stressful departure. Traveling with a pet is a giant decision and will impact both you and your pet greatly. Really ask yourself if your pet's life is better through travel or is it *your* life you're thinking about? If you answer no to the first question, perhaps you can find a new home for your pet.

Bikes

Depending on where you live, bikes are a great item to sell via craigslist or Facebook marketplace. They're often easy to get rid of and go to the first person. Bikes are also great items to donate to community centers and non-profits. If you have an unused bike, consider donating it to Toys for Tots at Christmas time.

Car

There are many ways to get rid of a car. You can donate it to National Public Radio or to an auto tech school. Maybe a family member wants it. Or, you can sell it privately or to a wholesaler like Carvana, Carmax or Vroom. See if you can time the selling of your car with your final ride to the airport. Your Estate Sellers can sell your car, if you'd like.

Paints, Toxic Chemicals, Fertilizer, Compacts Discs, Computers

You'll probably have to pay for disposal of these hazmat items like paints, chemicals, fertilizers, CDs, batteries, and computers. Although it's nice to think about donating computers to schools and clubs, make sure what you donate doesn't generate more work and cost for them. If the items are broken, just throw them away appropriately. Don't expect that a school can re-service your broken computer unless it's a trade school geared toward the tech and computer trades.

Mattresses

Depending on where you live, the Estate Seller may or may not be able to sell your mattress, and you may or may not be able to sell it in a garage sale or online. If they can't, you'll have to dispose of it on your large garbage pick up day. Or, there are several mattress recycling companies you can pay to pick up your mattresses. You'll need to do some research on how to get rid of your mattresses in your area. Try to recycle them, if possible.

Remainders

Remainders are everything that is left in the house after you've exhausted your best efforts to get rid of things. These include the odd hangars, the weird end table, the dog beds, clothing that didn't sell, leftover water bottles...all the odds and ends. There are a few choices on getting rid of the remainders.

1. Have a Free for All Open House like we did.
2. Bag it all up and throw it away.
3. Hire a remainder company to clean out the house

One Month to Departure: The Final Disposal of Stuff

While your departure date quickly approaches, if necessary, do the cosmetic work necessary on your house to sell it. Time this after the estate/garage sale if you can. You might need to paint the interior of the house, replace the carpeting, or spruce up the yard after people tromp through your house.

Checklist for Departure

Here is your checklist for getting out of your house. Your order might be different, but the action items are similar.

- Discuss nomad life idea
- Convince partner
- Determine finances
- Create budget
- Develop a credit card strategy
- Apply for necessary credit cards
- Think through banks and banking
- Establish tentative departure date
- Sign up for Trusted Housesitters and Liability Insurance
- Determine "how" you'll travel
- Evaluate rent vs sell options for home
- Set departure date
- Tell family
- Anticipate closing date for house
- Invite family and friends to house to take goods

- Contact Estate Sellers/Schedule garage sale
- Dispose of everything you don't need in the next six months
- Research Medical Insurance options
- Find out "extra garbage day"
- Set estate sale date
- List house
- Establish any new bank accounts
- Download bank and credit apps to phone
- Test money transfers between accounts
- Order debit cards
- Dispose of everything you don't need in the next three months
- Change mailing address on bank and credit card accounts
- Dispose of everything you don't need in the next month
- Have goodbye parties
- Have estate sale
- Have Free for All day
- Clean out house
- Put "extra garbage out"
- Show house
- Sell any remaining items
- Close on house
- Breathe
- Make any final trips to Goodwill
- Establish domicile
- Place items in safe deposit box and/or storage unit
- Sell car
- Activate Medical and Travel Insurance

- Get on plane

The Leaving Stage

You've worked a long list of action items, whittled all of your possessions down to your suitcases, and left your home. Now you must figure out how to get to where you're heading first. Going forward, you can concentrate on your life as a nomad: it is very different from your life as a stationary person. You need different tools to make your nomad life easy and livable.

We've separated these items out for simplicity, but you might be working these items in tandem with your Disposal Phase. Perhaps you can split the workload between you and your partner?

Domiciling and Residency

Getting your mail and having a place to call home, even if it isn't your home, is a big part of nomad life. You'll have to pick a state where you'll pay taxes and vote. When establishing your residency, it's important to ensure your story about where you live is consistent with your behavior. Even if you don't physically live in the place where your address is, you should at least have some allegiance to that address. Perhaps you join the local Rotary, get a library card, donate to the local shelter, or participate in a local club virtually. You may even have your doctors, accountants and future real estate agent on speed dial.

As a nomad, how do you establish domicile and residency? It depends on if you own or rent a home versus not owning or renting a home. We break it down for you.

If you own or rent a home:

If you want to continue holding on to your US citizenship, you'll need to establish residency and domicile in a state of your choosing. What's the difference between the two? Residency is where you live, and domiciling is where you vote and pay taxes. For example, you may domicile in New York where you vote, but you establish residency in Florida where you live for the winter. If you decide to keep your home and rent it out, you can likely keep your home's address as both your residency and your domicile.

If you don't own or rent:

If you don't own or rent, establishing domicile and residency can be quite tedious, and it will depend on the state and its rules. In order to establish either, you'll likely need a drivers license or a state ID from your selected state. In order to get that ID, most states require that you have an address. A utility bill or bank statement that proves your address helps you get your ID. Once you have an ID with a local address, you can register to vote. But if you don't have an address, there are a few options. There are three states that nomads find easiest to work with: South Dakota, Florida, and Texas. In addition, none of these three states charge state income tax, which might be an additional bonus for retirees. You'll want to research the particular tax issues for the state you pick.

If you have a friend or family member:

A route that many mobile people use to establish an address is to use the address of a family member or a friend. Their friend gathers their mail and monitors correspondence in your absence.

Getting Mail and Voting

Once you pick the state where you'll domicile, you'll need to figure out how to get your mail. There are many companies that will provide a mail service and an address for you to use for establishing your residency. Some states and banks will hiccup over these virtual services, making it difficult for you to get mail or to vote. Nonetheless, all the services basically work the same. You use their address as yours, they receive your mail, and they forward your mail per your instructions. In addition, most of them have a scanning service available, too. You can ask them to scan particular pieces of mail so that they never have to forward any hard copies of mail.

If you decide to use RV Escapees as your mail service and domicile in Texas, and in particular in Polk County like we did, here are the steps you must go through to be successful. The order is very particular and can't be modified. This order is probably similar in other states, too.

Note: All documents must show your current legal name and be original or certified copies. If your name differs, you must show legal documents supporting the name change

1. Sign up with RV Escapees and get an unique address.
2. When signing up, make sure you tell them we sent you so we get a referral credit. (Thank you!)

3. Make an appointment to get your Driver's License. At the time we made ours, the next available appointment was over two weeks away. You can make the appointment online at this website.

4. Change your address on your bank and credit card statements in time to have a monthly statement printed with your Texas address.

5. If you have a vehicle you'll register in Texas, get Texas auto insurance.

6. Get your car inspected. We used Kyle Thompson, 936-329-0839 (3224 E FM 1998, Goodrich, TX 77335). He's very familiar with RV Escapees and will help with your RV, too. At the inspection, you need to show proof of TX insurance and an IF of the car owner. It's okay if the ID is out of state.

7. Go to the Tax Assessor office (416 N Washington Ave, Livingston, TX) and register your vehicle. You will need the passed inspection slip, your TEXAS insurance, your ID and your current vehicle registration.

8. Go to your Drivers License appointment. (1737 N Washington Ave, Livingston, TX 77351, USA) Bring your car registration and TX car insurance (if you're registering a car), original or certified copy of your birth certificate, valid unexpired passport, employment authorization card or permanent residence card and your valid unexpired out-of-state drivers license which you will surrender. You also need to bring your social security card or something with your social security card number printed on it like a W2 or a 1040. Bring two proofs of TX residency. These can be bank statements from two different banks (see number 3 above.) Your cell phone bill is not a legitimate source. And finally, if you have a legal name change, you must bring those original documents, too.

9. While at the driver's license, you can ask to register to vote.

10. You might want to do the extra step of registering to vote at the Elections Office at Polk County Courthouse, 101 W Church St, Livingston, TX 77351. There you can also request your absentee ballot.

11. It will take about two weeks for your drivers license to arrive in the mail, so be sure you've planned ahead for how to get it. In the meantime, you'll have a temporary paper copy.

Buying Global Medical/Health Insurance

In order to buy Global Medical/Health Insurance, you can go to a broker or go directly to the insurance company's website. A broker often represents several different insurance company providers. If you go directly to the provider, they'll most likely just assign you a broker based on your zip code. If you go to a broker, you'll have someone to talk to and will help you sort out all the options. Follow these steps to find global medical insurance:

1. Confirm your current insurance policy doesn't cover you outside of the US.

2. Google "global medical insurance."

3. Sort through the results, focusing on the major providers like GeoBlue, IMG, Aetna, and Cigna.

4. Focus on the annual out-of-pocket deductible and total coverage amount.

5. Think about your pre-existing conditions. You can get coverage for these, but the more conditions you have, the more expensive the coverage.

6. Narrow down your choices to the top three plans.

7. Call their representatives and explain your scenarios. Ask questions about your conditions. Verify which countries you need coverage for.

8. Know your departure date. Your quotes are only good for 30 days prior to departure.

9. Triangulate the info among the three reps and have them run quotes for you.

10. Look at the links they send you of the quotes they run. Read all the fine print.

11. Set up a payment plan and purchase. Activate it for your departure date.

12. Download the ID card and coverage letters. Print them out. Put them in your "important papers" that you'll carry with you. Add them to a folder in the cloud so you have them digitally as well.

13. Consider if you need an additional Travel Policy to pick up COVID coverage and/or trip cancellation coverage. Purchase if necessary.

Finding Medical Care When You Travel

Although all countries will be different in how you access their health care, there are a few ways to start. We've used all of these when we've traveled, including in Russia, Hong Kong, China, Mexico, and Scotland.

1. If you have a global insurance provider, check their website for local providers. They may also have a hotline to dial to ask for where to seek care.

2. Ask your hotel concierge. If you're not staying at a swanky place with a concierge, go to one and tip the concierge.

3. Check the expat communities both virtually on Facebook and in public. You'll find expats at bars where NFL football is playing, at Starbucks, and at Thanksgiving dinner celebrations, among others.

4. Go to the local pharmacy. Likely, the pharmacist will speak English.

5. Go to an English teaching school. Speak to one of the local teachers who teaches English. Hire them, if necessary, to make phone calls and appointments for you.

6. Search the internet. Many medical clinics throughout the world cater to English-speaking travelers looking for medical care. Don't be shy to ask them what they charge and about how they specialize. Ask them for recommendations and referrals if they can't help you.

Prescriptions Abroad

Many countries are not as regulated about drugs and prescriptions as the US, and you can often buy your medicines over the counter. Examples of these include Prilosec, Viagra, Levitra, Various antibiotics, Birth control. You may need to set up an appointment with a local doctor to get your drugs filled at the local pharmacy, and often these appointments are very cheap.

The Nomad Travel Stage

Now that you've gotten rid of your stuff, figured out your insurance needs, managed your credit cards, and gotten on the road, you're ready to think about accommodation. Back when you were sorting through your stuff, you should have thought some of this through.

Thinking through Accommodations

Are you camping? Hoteling? Airbnbing? Maybe you're considering house sitting? Here's a few tips we've used:

Hotels

Make sure you're signed up for any hotel chain's reward program. When you're paying for lodging every night, your status and points will add up quickly. Additionally, when you sign up for credit cards that are attached to the hotel chains, you'll get additional rewards. We often use these free nights for special locations or in big cities where hotels are expensive.

Airbnb

When booking Airbnb, also double check if the same listing is on Booking.com, where you might save on the service fees. Also, be sure to book for more than 7 days or more than 28 days on Airbnb. This way, you'll get weekly and monthly discounts. It also can pay to contact the host directly to get better pricing if you've got a scenario that would encourage the host to reduce the price. Even if they won't reduce the price, you can always ask for other contingencies like better cancellation policies or later check out times.

1. Before getting on Airbnb, go to Google and research the neighborhood where you want to stay.
   a. Is it in a good location? Is it near gyms, groceries, transit, museums, stadiums, beach, mountains?
   b. Use the Google zoom tool to see the home at the street level. Is there traffic? Parking? Hospital nearby? Fire station? Sidewalks?
   c. Map distances from the center of the neighborhood to places you'll walk. Is the walk safe? Easy? Uphill?
   d. Find the zip/postal code of the ideal neighborhood or the name of the neighborhood.
2. Return to Airbnb with the zip/postal code or the neighborhood name. Begin your search with those data points.
3. Filter your search by date, price, bedrooms, and any other criteria important to you.
4. Narrow your choices to your top five.
   a. Review each choice. Look at the bed, the kitchen, and the shower. Are they the size you want and have the function and comfort you need?
   b. Don't select homes that have more than what you want. Do you really need a garage if you don't have a car? Pay for what you'll use.
   c. Use the zoom tools within Airbnb to scrutinize the location and street

5. Review the dates. If you stayed a day longer, would you get the weekly rate or the monthly rate? Airbnb gives discounts for 7 days and 28 days.

6. Review the cancellation policy. For all Airbnb reservations of 28 days or more, the cancellation policy is the same. It's free for 48 hours and then non refundable after 48 hours. Might your plans change?

7. If you're happy with the price and cancellation policy, book the reservation.

8. If you're unhappy, reach out to the host.

    a. If you're unhappy with the price, ask for a discount and explain why. You might say that you see many locations available for that week, that you travel full-time and you're trying to budget your expenses, that you really love the place, etc. Instead of asking for a discount, offer the price you're willing to pay.

    b. If you're unhappy with the cancellation policy, explain why. State you're concerned about travel changes, medical issues, political turmoil, etc. Ask for the cancellation policy you would like to have, for example: "Would you be willing to honor 100% cancellation up to one week prior to arrival?"

Tip: Delta has a partnership with Aibnb and you can get Delta SkyMiles from your Airbnb purchases. It's easy to set up. Start at www.delta.com/airbnb, add your Delta SkyMiles number, and then book your Airbnb. Be careful though. You'll want to double check rates both from the Delta site and from Airbnb. Sometimes the Delta site showed higher rates or didn't list a property at all.

Housesitting

Housesitting is a great way to lower your accommodation expenses, meet great people, hug super pets, and stay in places you might not normally find. We recommend using the website Trusted Housesitters, and here are some tips on how to get your first house sit where it's a mutual exchange of services. You stay for free, and the homeowner doesn't pay for pet care.

Get Great Housesits

To get the good housesits, you have to have three things:

1. A great profile and great application
2. Great 5-star reviews
3. A unique identifier that home owners appreciate

When applying for housesits, the homeowners have three concerns that you need to overcome in order to get the housesit. They fear the following things:

1. Their pets getting ignored and not getting the care they need.
2. Their home getting trashed.
3. Their housesitters canceling at the last minute or leaving mid sit.

Create a Killer Profile

Create your profile with these concerns in mind. In your profile, express your personality and why you are traveling. If you have a particular mission (to work in dog shelters, for example), include that. Be sure you are relatable to the people who you want to house sit for. Many homeowners also love to travel, which is why they look for house sitters. They might also have a love of language, food, and culture. Express your love for these things, too. Build camaraderie.

Create a Killer Application

When you apply to the sit, address trust issues by giving examples of your reliability and your commitment to the sit. If you have 5-star reviews, point that out in your application. If you don't have any reviews yet, mention other places where you might be well reviewed like on Airbnb or in Google Reviews. Explain where you're coming from and how they can rely on you to be at their home in time. Offer to have a zoom call.

Create a Killer Zoom

On your zoom, address the "trashing of the house" issue by indirectly letting them see where you are in the zoom. If you're at a housesit, make sure the background in your zoom is clean and tidy. If you're in your home, try to show a clean kitchen or a tidy living room. Mention that you will leave the home clean. Ask if there's a washer/dryer so you can wash the sheets and towels before leaving. If there are pets where you currently are, invite them into the zoom so the homeowners can see your interaction with other pets.

Also on the zoom, ask how often they want to be communicated with. Do they need pictures every day, twice a day, or just once a week? Also discuss how often you'll communicate with each other prior to arriving. Even if your housesit is months away, drop a note about your logistics or a picture of a pet at a current sit so they know you're thinking of them and still planning on coming their way. This communication develops trust and opens lines for chatting and discussion.

Get 5-star Reviews

Once you nail the housesit, the hard work has just begun. While on the housesit, be sure to follow the homeowners' instructions, communicating along the way. Send pictures of happy pets having happy experiences. Enjoy your stay, meet the locals, eat the cuisine, and exercise the pets as requested. When it's time for the homeowner to arrive, make sure you have relieved as much stress as you can. They'll be tired from traveling and excited to see their pets, so how can you make their return to their home more enjoyable?

1. Make sure it's *cleaner* than how you found it in the places that you use. You don't have to deep clean the entire house, but definitely make sure the bedroom, bathroom, kitchen and living space are better than you found them, which includes clean sheets, emptied trash, and smudge free surfaces.

2. Pick up dog poop, empty the litter box, and change the cages.

3. If the yard needs tidying, do it, including mowing, trimming, leaf raking.

4. Lay out the mail and packages neatly.

5. If it makes sense, have a meal ready for them. If you're not a good cook or can't cook due to logistics, have something pre-made in the refrigerator, time a delivery from Uber Eats, or at least have a lasagna in the freezer.

Create A Unique Identifier

Finally, to secure that 5-star review, do something unique. Leave fresh flowers and/or bake a special treat. If you do bake something, be sensitive to their diet needs which you can discover by reviewing the flours and sugars they keep in their cabinets. Draw a pet portrait. Find something that draws on your personality and makes you both memorable and relatable so that it's called out in the review the homeowner will write.

How to Book Lodging

With your flights booked, you'll want to look again at housing. Maybe you have all of your accommodation covered with housesitting, or maybe you need to fill the time between your housesits with Airbnbs or hotels.

Here's the process we recommend when you book your next lodging arrangement.

1. Set an alert in <u>Trusted Housesitters</u> for your chosen location.
2. Let time pass and watch, wait, and hope that the perfect house sit will come up. We've booked some housesits up to four months out, but now we wait a bit longer.
3. Search Airbnb for your perfect accommodation.
4. Search Booking.com as well. Look for the same property that might be on Airbnb and is also on Booking. See if the prices and cancellation policies differ. Pick the better one.
5. If you want to stay in a hotel, search for a room on Hotels.com and then compare the same room on the hotel's website.
6. If going the hotel route, go to Chase.com (or equivalent credit card website) and find the same hotel room. Compare price vs points vs the hotel's website. Determine which is the better option.
7. About a month prior to traveling, if you haven't found a housesit, book your Airbnb. Note that on Airbnb, you can get better rates if you book a week or a month at a time. Sadly, the cancellation policy is very bad for monthly rentals on Airbnb, so be sure you are firm on your plans.

Long-Leg Travel and Transit

Once you've thought through some of your accommodation strategy and maybe even booked a few housesits, you'll want to start thinking about your long-leg travel and how to book it. Long-leg travel is those segments of your air travel that are longer than 3-4 hours and likely cross continents. Repositioning cruises can also be long-leg travel.

Long Flights or Repositioning Cruises

When booking long-leg travel, follow these steps to determine how and where to purchase our tickets. You'll use these steps to also help you determine if you should fly or use a repositioning cruise. Repositioning cruises are one-way cruises that cruise lines use to get their boats positioned for new travel seasons. You can take advantage of these types of cruises to cross oceans and continents at about the same price you'd pay if you flew and paid for accommodation.

1. Check Skyscanner.com for an approximate price of an airline ticket.
2. Evaluate if other days of the week are cheaper or have better routing.
3. Find the airline that has the cheapest price overall (including baggage fees).
4. If you have time, set a price alert on Kayak.com or Skyscanner.com.
5. Go to the airline's website and check prices and routing for paying in cash and with points
6. Go to cruises.com and check if there is a repositioning cruise available. These are often called "trans-Atlantic" or "trans-Pacific" cruises.
7. Do the math to determine if the cruise is a good deal versus flying and paying for hotel nights, food, entertainment, etc.

8. Check both the flights and the cruise prices on chase.com (or equivalent other credit card) in their travel reward section.

9. Determine if it's better to pay cash or use travel points to pay on the credit card website.

10. Pull all the data points together: cruise price, flight+hotel+food price, credit card points "price", airline and/or cruise points "price."

11. Determine which credit card to use based on where you'll get the best points multipliers.

12. Confirm that the credit card you'll use has the travel insurance policy you need for the trip.

13. Make a purchase. This purchase will be at one of three places: the airline website, the cruise line website, or the credit card website.

Tip: Never book overseas tickets through a travel agent such as Travelocity, Cruisecritic, or AAA. When your flight gets delayed and you're sitting in the airport trying to make new arrangements, your airline will not talk to you if you have booked through a third party. You have to go through the third party to get rebooked. This becomes a giant hassle if time zones are involved, if your cell phone doesn't have a good international plan, or you have to wait until the proper person is available.

The Nomad Day-to-Day Living Stage

In your nomad day-to-day living stage, you'll be living your life. Some days you'll go do an activity in your new location, perhaps taking in a walking tour or a museum. Other days, you'll find yourself on your computer, paying bills, communicating with family, or planning your next destination. Here are some tips for what to do in your nomad day-to-day life.

Passports, Visas, and Paperwork

Managing your important documents takes time, and you always want to be sure you have digital copies in the cloud.

Passport: When you get your next passport, make sure to ask for extra pages. They're free, and you'll use them. Make a copy of your picture page and your signature page. Trim them to actual size and then laminate them together. Use the copy to show as ID when you check into places. Most places will take copies, but have your original handy, especially for border crossings. Keep the original in a water-proof ziploc, and make sure a digital copy is in the cloud.

Visas: Plan ahead for the Visas you might need as you travel. Most of the time, you can only get a Visa if you have your accommodation and travel information. Sometimes you can get Visas when you arrive. Carry an extra passport photo with you because some Visas require a photo. Finding a place to take a passport photo can be a challenge.

Visas in the European Union

For US citizens, the Visa game is changing in 2022 for the European Union (EU). At that point, we'll actually have to go online and register at ETIAS.. But up until then, the rules for visiting the EU are the same. Here's the basic breakdown.

The EU is a set of countries. Within the EU is an area called the Schengen Zone. All countries within the Schengen Zone belong to the EU but not all EU countries are in the Schengen Zone. US citizens who want to visit the Schengen Zone can only be within the Schengen Zone for 90 days total over a rolling 180-day time frame. Here is an example:

January 1. Arrive in France. Stay 30 days,
February 1. Leave France and go to Spain for 28 days.
March 1. Leave Spain. Go go Portugal for 31 days.
April 1. You must be out of the Schengen Zone for 90 days before you can stay another day.
April 1. Go to Ireland, Croatia, and England. Stay 90 days.
July 1. Return to Schengen. Repeat.

You can always and only be in Schengen for 90 days or less at one time even if your rolling 180 days breaks between the 90 days. Your rolling 180 days rolls with you. To see the lists of Schengen and non-Schengen countries, take a look at the Schengen website. It's excellent and helps answer all the Schengen scenarios. You might also want to download the Schengen calculator to help you keep track of your Schengen dates.

The US State Department's website is good for checking where you need visas. You can also go to the website of the county-in-question, too, but often the information will be in the local country's language. At the State Department website, you can also check for current COVID requirements and other danger levels within a country.

Important Paperwork to Carry with You

Carry with you the following docs and also put digital copies in the cloud:

- Any prescriptions
- COVID cards
- Marriage license
- Legal documents regarding name changes
- Insurance IDs
- Insurance Coverage Letters

Money, Cash, Credit Cards

Getting, having and maintaining your money and access to money can be a bit of a magician's trick as you travel around the world. There are a few tried-and-true strategies you should maintain in order to always have access to your money. Below are general rules that we follow as we travel. They can vary a bit by country, but they have always worked for us as we travel.

You must understand that at least one of two of the following things WILL happen to you as you travel, so you must have an activated plan all the time for when any of them happen.

1. Your credit card will go fraud.
2. You will get robbed.

3.   You will lose your id/wallet/credit card/phone.

Money Basics as You Travel

Some countries will want cash, some will only accept credit cards. In general, the Americas (except for Canada and the US) want cash, Europe, Australia and New Zealand want credit cards, and everywhere else is a hodgepodge. Thus, if you're going to travel the world, you need to be prepared for all types of currency economies. Therefore, you'll need the following tools.

1.   Three debit cards from three different accounts and preferably three different banks.

2.   Three different credit cards from three different accounts and preferably three different banks

3.   Three different forms of ID from government-issuing agencies.

Why three? I'll get into that shortly.

When to Use your Debit Card

You will use your debit cards at ATMs to get cash. That's it. You will most likely not be able to use your debit card at points of purchase. They are unreliable at these places and cause more headache than necessary. Even if your debit card has a chip, and even if your debit card has a PIN, and even if you can run your debit card as a credit card, odds are it won't work. In our experiences, whenever we try to use our debit cards at a point-of-purchase scenario, they will go fraud. Getting a debit card replaced while traveling is quite a hassle. More on that later.

When to Use your Credit Card/Phone/Contactless

You will use your credit card everywhere that you can't or don't use cash. This includes the grocery, services, hotels, taxis, buses, travel, and online. If it "only" costs $1, use your credit card. Use it, use it, use it. Your credit card is the work horse in your wallet. Carry it with you at all times.

If possible, and we highly encourage this, link your credit cards to your phone via Google Pay, Apple Pay or Samsung Pay and use your phone for credit purchases. Contactless phone charges work all over Europe, and they work well in the Americas where they are accepted. By using your credit card, you facilitate transactions more smoothly, you can track all your expenses, and you can get credit card rewards that add up to free travel rewards. You rarely need a PIN to use your credit card, and you must have a chip card for success. Additionally, when you replace your credit card, the bank will automatically update your credit in your digital wallet, giving you access to the new card before you actually get the physical card in the mail.

How Many Debit/Credit Cards Should You Have

You should carry with you three complete sets of cards. What's a set? A debit card, a credit card with no international transaction fees, and an ID. Because you will have fraud, lose your wallet/phone, or get robbed, you need to just plan ahead for these events. By having three sets, you're assured you can get through the trauma and drama of getting these important documents replaced.

Why Three Wallets?

You should always have two credit cards with you. Randomly, one will not work. It just happens. It will not work at one vendor but it will work at

TWO CARRY-ONS AND A PLAN

another. In this case, you can use your backup. But if one of the two gets lost/stolen/fraud, you don't have a backup. Thus, carry three sets.

Why Three IDs?

IDs are probably the hardest things to replace internationally. Generally, you can't call up the DMV and have them send you a copy to an international address. Losing your passport is triply difficult and most often requires a trip to an embassy. These actions take time and money, which are both hard to come by when you don't have credit cards or IDs to help you get them. Having three IDs on hand creates the redundancy you need to get things replaced. For extra security, always have a backup set of passport photos in your backpack. If you lose your passport or need to get a Visa on the fly, you'll have passport photos handy.

How to Get Cash

Getting cash can be a challenge because it can be hard to find ATMs and because ATMs, especially in cash-based cultures, are often empty. Here are some tips for how to get cash:

1. Use the airport ATM, preferably the one associated with a bank.
2. Use your bank debit card (your ATM card), not your credit card at the ATM. If you use your credit card to get cash, it's considered a cash advance and you will immediately be charged high interest rates by your bank on the cash advance.
3. Get enough money to get through a few days. This amount is based on where you will need to spend cash rather than a credit card. In Europe, you need very little cash. In Mexico, you need a lot of cash. Don't withdraw more than you need for 3-4 days. If you use a Schwab

card, there are no transaction and ATM fees, so there's no fear of racking up ATM fees for multiple withdrawals.

4. Pick a well-lit, well-situated ATM that belongs to a bank and has lots of people using it.

5. When the ATM asks you if you want the withdrawal computed in local currency or in dollars, always say local currency.

6. Withdraw the cash and count it on camera to ensure you get the amount you requested.

7. Immediately split the cash with your partner and/or put some in your wallet, some in your suitcase, and some in your backpack. If you get robbed, they won't get all of it.

8. Before leaving the airport, use your cash to buy a bottle of water. Make sure you get coins and small bills for change. You'll need it for bus fares and tips.

Tools of Nomad Life

We recommend the following tools and gear.

Cell phone:

We recommend Pixel for its ease of use and killer camera.

Cell phone service:

Google Fi. If you decide to go the Sim route, you'll have to 1) find a provider, 2) buy the Sim card, 3) pray it works, 4) possibly struggle in the local language and 5) have high levels of frustration. We pay Google's fees happily instead of trying to save $10-20 monthly on our cell phone bill. A couple of things to know about Google Fi:

1. You must have a US-based phone number
2. You have to start service while you're in the US
3. There are rumors about Google throttling your service after six months of continued service out of the country. We have yet to have this happen to us.
4. If you have a Pixel phone, you get free storage in Google Photos in the cloud.

You can use Google Fi for about six months outside of the USA. If you stay longer than six consecutive months, Google will cut you off of your data until you return to the US. This happened to us. We also found that trying to "reset" your Google Fi clock by returning to the USA for a few days only delays the six-month deadline. You have to stay in the USA for at least six months for your data clock to reset.

Flexiroam after Google Fi. Thus, once we ran out of our Google Fi time, we turned to a different solution. We ported our Google Fi phone numbers to Google Voice so we'd keep our USA numbers. We then used the global data plan from Flexiroam. They have an e-SIM card, so we didn't have to wait for a SIM card to arrive. We downloaded the Flexiroam app, changed a few settings, and we are up and running. Flexiroam has online sales for data all the time. We got 11G of global data for $65, and it must be used within 360 days. The data is also shareable with other Flexiroam users. Use our Flexiroam code to get 100M free when you start with a new plan.

Computers:

Dell Inspirion 13 5000. The small size is perfect to slip into a backpack and to use on an airline drop-down tray.

WIFI Router and VPN Service:

This one for the router and Cyberghost VPN. for VPN Service

E-Reader:

Kindle Paperwhite. Subscribe to Freebooksy.com, a free service, where you can get access to free ebooks every day.

Camera:

Use your phone. Unless you're a professional photographer, there's no need to carry special gear that's heavy and that you need to have to worry about getting thieved.

WhatsApp:

A free communications app where you can text, video call, and call for free when on wifi. The entire world outside of the US uses it. The person you want to reach must also use WhatsApp, which is highly likely throughout the world.

Google Translate:

Great for on-the-fly chatting while in the country. The disadvantage is that you must have an internet connection to use it.

Spanish Dict:

A super app for English to Spanish and Spanish to English. It does not require an internet connection to use.

How to Find Nomad Friends

Making friends while traveling is important. You can't rely 100% on your partner or yourself for everything. Here are a few ways to find nomad friends:

1. On Facebook in the following groups:
    a. Go With Less
    b. Senior Nomads
    c. Full-time Nomads
2. In airports and train stations at the gates going to your destinations.
3. Although we rarely frequent American-branded restaurants and coffee shops, it is easy to find English-speaking compadres there. Look to Starbucks particularly.
4. Even if you don't plan to stay in hostels, hostels are great places to find full-time travelers. Hostels often have group events open to the public. These are great places to make new friends.
5. On cruises, make friends at shared dinner tables, through on-board events and games or competitions.

What to Do Each Day

Before arriving or right after you arrive, research things to do by doing the following:

1. Prior to arriving, join the relevant Facebook groups for the area. There is usually an Expat group, but there are often other groups named after neighborhoods or things you like to do. For example, look for "Vegans in XX". By searching on a topic, you'll find things the locals are doing. It's a bonus if you can search in the local language.

2.   Google "Fun Things to Do in XX" or "Free Things to Do in XX". Almost always, there will be a TripAdvisor post with this content. Although TripAdvisor is good for the Top 10 Things to Do, it's very basic and touristy. Rather, add "blog" to the search and find local bloggers who have their own, non-commercial spin on their town. In addition, look at Culture Trip's report as well.

3.   Find the "Free Walking Tour" that's available in the area and schedule this for the first couple of days of arrival. This gives you the lay of the land and likely takes you to the Top Ten attractions in an area.

4.   At the walking tour, make friends with the attendees and the guide. Ask your new friends to grab a drink afterward and hopefully the guide will join you. Always treat the guide. Even if these meetings don't create friendships, they likely will produce additional things to do.

5.   In the first week of arriving, use Facebook again to search for events. Facebook seems to be better at serving up events when you're physically in the location when Facebook can use location services tools to provide content.

6.   Once you find an event on Facebook, click the Going button and go. If you're not sure if you'll go, click Maybe. The Maybe tells Facebook to serve you up additional, similar events that might be attractive to you. It also tells the host of the event of your interest, and the host might reach out as well.

7.   Search Eventbrite.com for things to do. Often, free events require tickets and Eventbrite will have them.

8.   Join a gym when you arrive, too. Try to find the local community center, as the atmosphere in these places generally seems friendlier to meeting strangers. People don't seem so rushed.

9. If you join a commercial gym, negotiate with the gym owner to pay only for the time you will be there. Rather than buy a month's membership, try to negotiate for 10 workouts, for example. Sometimes the memberships or drop-in fees are so cheap, you won't need to negotiate.

10. At the gym, arrive early or stay late after a class to try and meet people. Often, they want to practice their English. Give a verbal "high five" to someone during a workout. This breaks the ice and will allow for conversation. Ask people about local things to do and places to go. This, too, opens up conversation. Although it's easier to do online workouts with YouTube, etc, it's more rewarding, socially, to get to the gym.

11. Find hiking and walking clubs through Meetup. Locals know the trails and can't be beat for understanding and sharing safety and navigation tips. Saturday mornings are often the best times to just show up at trailheads and join others or hike near them.

12. Ask the local butcher or produce seller for how to cook something. This not only helps you practice your language, but the next time you buy, you'll have a soft opening to the next conversation. This might open up a dinner invite!

13. Volunteer at the local food bank. Be gentle with the guests at the food bank where you'll be able to practice the local language, and make friends with the other volunteers.

14. Go to a Rotary Club meeting. Every town in the world seems to have one, and they are generally open to anyone. Introduce yourself and tell them your interest. Rotarians have a mission to improve the world, and you can help them.

15. Show up to the local ball court or field. See if you can get invited into a pickup game of basketball or football, or ask if they'll teach you the

local game such as Gaelic football or cricket. Even if you don't want to play, stay and watch. Ask a local about a rule of the game or who a favorite team might be. Find the local professional version of the game and attend a match.

16. Read the bulletin boards at the grocery or in your housing complex. See if there's something you can join or help with.

17. Talk to your homeowner if you're a pet sitting or your Airbnb host. See if they are in walking groups and ask if you can join their friends while they are out of town. If they volunteer someplace, ask if you can do their responsibility for the duration of your stay.

18. If you're staying in a country that has pub culture, go to the pub. Relax and listen to the music. Chat up the person next to you.

19. Do something new. We googled "sheep trials" and attended a sheep herding event. We knew nothing of what was going on and had great fun asking the locals about it.

20. Write and share your experiences. Whether via a blog or social media, trust the interactions from others and engage. They will reap rewards and camaraderie.

21. Search Meetup for groups that have your interest and attend a meeting.

Have Fun

We hope we've given you the tools to start your full-time traveling adventure. Maybe you won't go full-time, or maybe you'll just head out for a few months at a time. No matter what you do, we hope you travel a little lighter, a little farther, and a little bit happier as you enjoy your adventure in the world. Have fun. And if you're in our neck of the woods this week, reach out. We'd love to share a cuppa with you.

About the Author

Chris Englert has been traveling and writing her entire life. From her first school project about Czechoslovakia in fifth grade to her latest book, she can't remember never not thinking nor writing about traveling. She and her husband, Steve, travel the world with their two carry-on bags, making memories daily, and sharing annoying pictures of their smiling faces to their family and friends often. Carrying everything she owns in her carry-on and her daypack, she enjoys promoting peace through the friends she makes and goes to sleep at night hoping she made the world a better place that day.

Other books by Chris Englert

Travel Magic Postcards: Vignettes from the Walking Traveler

Walking Denver's Neighborhoods

Best Urban Hikes: Denver

Discovering Denver's Parks: A Locals Guide

Two Carry-Ons and a Plan: Traveling as Full-Time Nomads

50 Hikes 50 States: A Couple's Journey to Hike the USA

www.EatWalkLearn.com

Please subscribe to our newsletter.

Index

Made in the USA
Las Vegas, NV
02 November 2024

11022528R00089